ZIMBOLICIOUS ANTHOLOGY VOL 9:

An Anthology of Zimbabwean Literature and Arts

Edited by Tendai Rinos Mwanaka

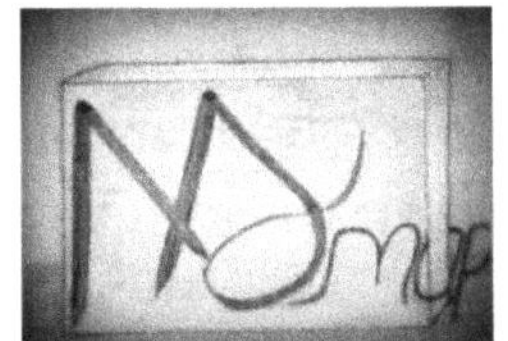

Mwanaka Media and Publishing Pvt Ltd,
Chitungwiza Zimbabwe
*
Creativity, Wisdom and Beauty

Publisher: *Mmap*
Mwanaka Media and Publishing Pvt Ltd
24 Svosve Road, Zengeza 1
Chitungwiza Zimbabwe
mwanaka@yahoo.com
mwanaka13@gmail.com
www.africanbookscollective.com/publishers/mwanaka-media-and-publishing
https://facebook.com/MwanakaMediaAndPublishing/

Distributed in and outside N. America by African Books Collective
orders@africanbookscollective.com
www.africanbookscollective.com

ISBN: 978-1-77934-543-1
EAN: 9781779345431

DISCLAIMER
All views expressed in this publication are those of the author and do not necessarily reflect the views of *Mmap*.

Table of Contents

About editor

Tendai Rinos Mwanaka is a multidisciplinary artist, writer, musician, editor, publisher and producer with over 70 individual books and curated anthologies published in US, Northern Ireland, UK, Cameroon and Zimbabwe. He has 5 music albums, with new album, *For Mberikwazvo: The Winter After* (2025) recently released and his music is playing in at least 18 radio stations in US, Canada, UK, France, Israel, Brazil and Australia. He has hundreds of paintings and drawings, thousands of photographs, some exhibited, published and sold. His pieces have appeared in over 500 journals in over 35 countries and his books and writing is translated into at least 11 languages. His music can be licensed here: https://www.songtradr.com/tendai.mwanaka. And find him here: https://m.facebook.com/tendai.mwanaka

Contributor's Bio Notes

.

Ayanda Valeria Sithole an author from Bulawayo Zimbabwe who delves in poetry, penned effortlessly stylish with emotion and enamelled with raw imagination. *Maverick Thoughts, She Wrote...,Love Tendencies* and *Under The Sun* carry a storm of her literary works. She has featured in anthologies such as *Mercy and Poetic Healing, Voiced in Verses, Zimbolicious Anthology Volume 8* and *Poetritis Nirvana.*

Born August 1994 to agrarian parents in rural Marondera, under chief Nenguwo, **Beniah Takunda Munengwa** grew up to a blended urban and rural environment in a family of two. He is a graduate holder of the Bachelor of Applied Arts and Special Hons Degree from the University of Zimbabwe. He has a strong passion for words and is a columnist for *NewsDay* Zimbabwe, where he scribbles on issues to do with literature. To his name, is a number of unpublished poems and essays.

My name is **Rejoice Tavonga Makunda.** I am a twenty-year-old female who started writing at the age of 12. I am a law student at the University of Zimbabwe who just finished her first year. Becoming an author is a dream l have lived with for the longest time. I pray and wish l will 1 day be able to publish my novels and poems for public pleasure.

I'm **Tanea Nyika**, an 18-year-old female high school student from Zimbabwe with a remarkable talent and creativity when it comes to writing and storytelling. Despite juggling my academic pursuits, I have already achieved the extraordinary feat of publishing three novels by the age of 17 among which one is a poetry anthology, *Scarred Words.* My personal literary prowess and dedication to my craft have garnered attention both locally and internationally. As I prepare to graduate this year, the world eagerly anticipates the next captivating book in my burgeoning writing career.

David Chasumba is a Zimbabwean Writer and Poet. He has published two short story collections with Carnelian Heart Publishing: 2023 NAMA award winning, *The Mad Man on First Street and Other Short Stories (2022)* and *Behind the Façade and Other Stories (2024).* David's poems have been published by Kalahari Review, Ipikai Poetry Journal, British Haiku Society anthology (2023), in *Best "New" African Poets (2023)* anthology and in *MEN: An*

International Anthology of African and Latin American Writers, Volume 3. David lives in Bexhill-on sea, East Sussex, UK. X: @davidchasumba22

Simbarashe Andrew Kashiri developed a love for poetry at an early age and some of his earlier pieces were published by the now defunct *Moto Magazine* under the pseudonym Gumpet Munyori and Simbarashe G. Munoyori, as well as his own government name by the age he was 16. He has honed his craft over a period of almost 3 decades, however he now only writes when he wants to and feels inspired to do so. He takes delight in writing deep, meaningful poetry which can have varying interpretations, and using colorful explosive language.

Panashe Goneso: I have taken up the name "ProGressive linGuist" in the hopes that my work would be that; a language so progressive it effects changes and inspires many to be the change in their society. The time is now for the youths to take up the mantle and effect the change they want; I turn to pen and paper in the hopes that my pen will lead them. It is time for us to shape the narrative of our Zimbabwe, the awakening Giant.

Gamuchirai Susan Muchirahondo: Gamuchirai, better known as Susan in the literature field, is a young writer who has been writing for over 15 years now. She mainly writes raw emotional poetry that focuses on tragic romances, mental health, and death. She also writes short stories and children's books.

Placidia Chiwita is a simple girl from Harare, who has always been avid reader. It came as no surprise to those who knew her when she decided to start writing. She has written short stories and also published one novel titled Poisoned Passion.

Chenjerai Mhondera is a rabbi, a dissident reporter, Lord of controversies, a proofreader, editor, book reviewer and a previewer. He's a highly anthologised Writecian and a Globet; published in over two hundred-and-eighty publications -independent publications, anthologies, magazines, journals, newspapers; with different publishing houses both locally and internationally. Among the countries he's published, include Zimbabwe, South Africa, Cameroon, Nigeria, India, USA, Latin America, and or Serbia. His works have got several media reviews and coverage - both locally and internationally. He has won several literary awards and certificates. He's identified with originating and or inventing a new form of writing called HiCoup - and can identify with all its forms. He's also credited for discovering the 13th month of the year and creating his own calendar as well as being famed for raising the strong objections against the conventional letters of the alphabet and inconsistencies in the language, English. He's the world's favourite for interviews. He belongs to many writers' organisations or associations in Africa, and Africa beyond. His rejection of two international awards as contained in his controversial letter of rejection has generated so much controversies in the public and media circles.

Oscar Gwiriri is a Zimbabwean published in more than 60 books, both fiction and text books. His two books *Hatiponi* and *Chitima nditakure* were NAMA awards nominees in 2019. He is a Certified Forensic Investigations Professional (CFIP) and a Certified Information Systems Security Professional (CISSP). He also holds a *Master of Science in Strategic Management Degree, Bachelor of Business Administration, Associates of Arts in Business Administration, Diploma in Logistics and Transport (CILT, UK), Diploma in Workplace Safety and Health, Commanding United Nations Peacekeeping Operations Certificate*, and many other professional qualifications. He likes writing in his vernacular language (Shona) most.

Bradley Nsukuzokuduma Moyo is a writer from Bulawayo. His penname Brvdley The WordPill emanates from his mantra, 'pouring the poetic balm to heal the world.' He is an advocate for mental health and social justice. Bradley is a two time nominee for the second edition of the Poetry Red Carpet Awards where he was nominated for Best New artist and Best Page Poet. He has also partook in short story competitions and has published a short collection of poems which is titled Collateral, which is available online. His works has been featured on The Standard newspaper, Chronicle and other electronic media.

Matthew Kunashe Chikono is a short story writer and editor from Chitungwiza, Zimbabwe. He has edited anthologies such as *Zimbolicious Volume 8* and The rules of the city. He has published two solo short story collections *Dreams of Paradise* and *Blue threads and other stories.* His third book *Shreds* novella is currently in production

Boniface Matemba born 1981 in Harare Zimbabwe .Studied at the National Art Gallery visual arts studios .I express myself through painting and sculpting. I finishing my Art studies in 2003. My work is inspired by nature and is modern, semi abstract, simplified, social, different textures and movement .My subject is human figs, plants and animals

Jabulani Mzinyathi born on 01 September 1965 is a poet / novelist. He has several published poetry collection and a chiShona experimental novel. He is an avid reader too. Jabulani is a reggae fan who is greatly influenced by Peter Tosh, his favourite artiste. Jabulani is a former teacher, ex Magistrate and is currently is a lawyer in private practice based at Beitbridge , Zimbabwe .He is a human capital manager and is also a change management practitioner. He vows to keep on reading writing.

.

Introduction

As per our tradition for the past 9 years, we have compiled and edited another collection of Zimbabwean literature and arts, Zimbolicious Anthology Vol 9, from the entries we received from Zimbabwean writers and artists in 2024. This anthology as usual is open to any artist of Zimbabwean descent who works in literature and visual arts. In this anthology we have 6 prose pieces, several sculptures, installations and mixed media artworks from two artists, 12 poets and 12 photographs

Biniface Matemba with his arresting land sculptures begins the book, celebrating women as the light that moves the home forward. Hosea Tokwe's short story highlights the hustles Zimbabweans, especially Hararians deal with day to day to earn a living and the problems they face with authority, which you can also see mirrored in poetry by Makunda, Gwiriri, and photography by Mwanaka.

Several other artworks by Matemba are centred on animal sculpture, which is the heart of Zimbabwean sculpture in general, where animals are highlighted and that space between humans and animals take special space in an artist. Nyika starts the chorus on death for the next batch of stories and essays. She focus on abuse in the marital plane and how the character dies in the middle of changing vows with his partner, Chikono lights on drought, which we are currently grappling with, how it affected the life of the characters and their ability to achieve on their ambitions, maybe opening a vista in which the character might proceed with their ambition through the death of his grandfather which would free him from being beholden to the place. Chiwita highlights the ever pervading Cancer problem that now bedevils us, but gave it a light touch by creating a funeral in the form of celebrating the character when still alive...even though she is dying. Mwanaka uses dust as theory as he reminisces about his time at school, focusing on how mourning is personal. And the last prose piece that's coupled with installations and mixed media from Kucherera is an appreciation of Murehwa based artist Muvezvwa.

Part two of the book focuses on poetry and photography, with past contributors; Gwiriri, Mzinyathi, Mhondera, Muchirahondo, Munengwa, Muchuri, Sithole, Chasumba, being joined by a glut of new bloods to the family, covering a motley lot of topics, from politics, democracy, governance, love, death, religion, tradition, spirituality etc..., and these poems are aided by Mwanaka's haphazard photographs that touches on service delivery, piracy of photography, marriage, the fauna and flora, the city- as a space of economic activity, delusions and illusions...

Zimbolicious 9 is a potpourri of art, thoughts and intentions of Zimbabweans and how they keep going on despite several problems and a celebration of their identities. It is another meaningful contribution to Zimbabwean arts and the Zimbolicious identity.

Part 1: Prose, Sculptures, Installations and Mixed Media

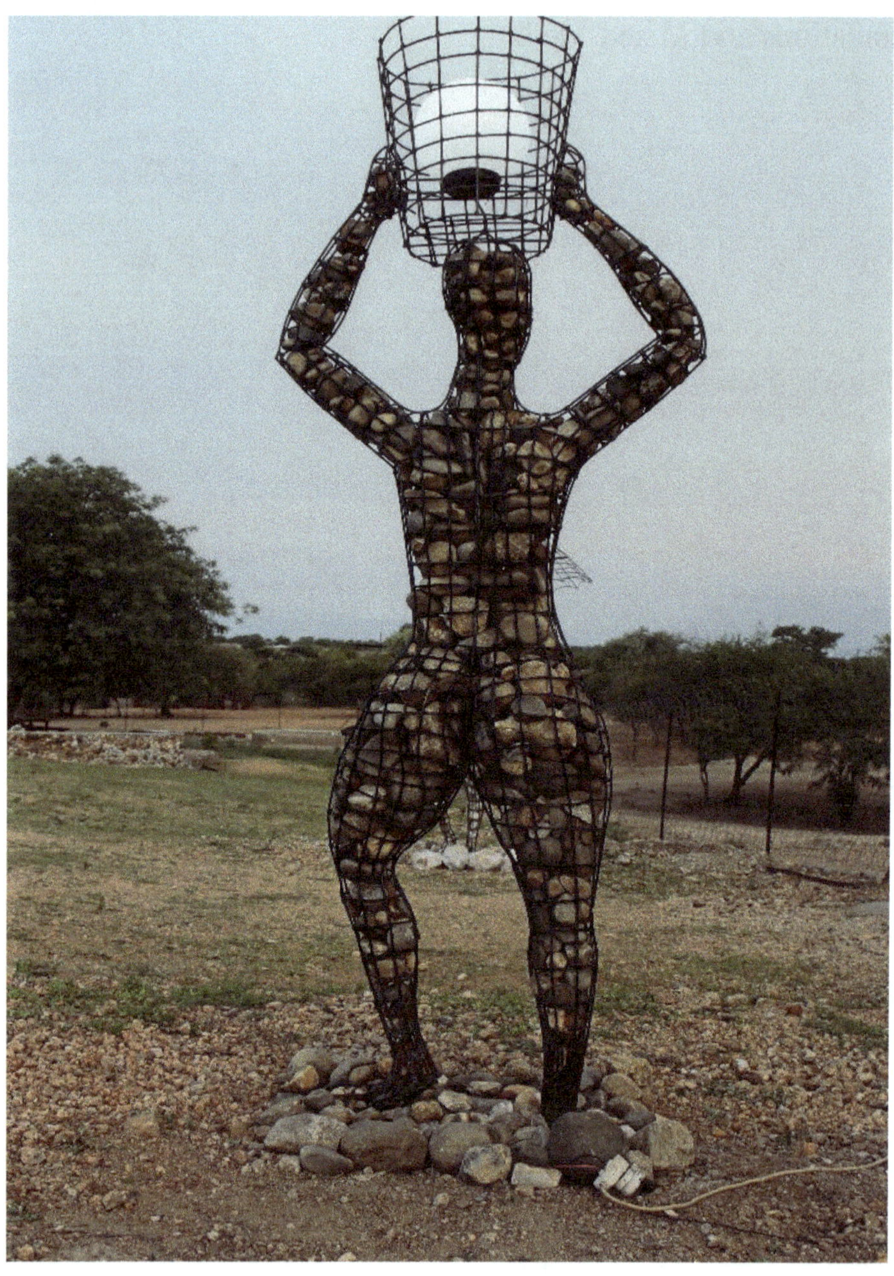

The Mother's Light

Boniface Matemba

Mother's light is a sculpture that also serves as a lighter. It is a mother carrying light above her head the same way mothers carry buckets of water on their heads. The sculpture is made of round bars and stones

Hustling - the daily struggle in Harare

Hosea Tokwe

July 2024

Piyo threw away the blankets from his springy bed alarmed by the intense brightness of the light spreading in his room. He hurriedly put on his black track suit bottom with yellow stripes and a grey tshirt. Retrieving his dirty canvas shoes underneath the bed he cursed himself for being late again knowing full well that this was a big blow to his meagre budget. To make matters worse for the third time he was wearing the same clothes again. How demeaning. But there was nothing he could do to improve his looks and outlook. The populace had become impoverished and he was not spared either. In today's fast life of hustling no one bothered to ask anybody's dressing and sense of decorum. How Piyo had fitted into this kind of life went without question. Life moved on.

Piyo checked his wrist watch once again. Surely, by now it was too late catching the much cheaper transport. He had nobody to blame but himself for his troubles.

He now stood up thinking deeply as he reflected on the long journey that he had traveled. A journey of hardship in a country whose economic meltdown had become the talk of the region, where struggling people came face to face with debilitating poverty.

Since completing his higher secondary school studies, Piyo had not secured a place at any of the local Universities neither could he afford the fees. His mother despite working at a government institution had openly advised him that she could not afford the tuition fees. For three months he had tried to post his curriculum vitae to different companies, sending unsolicited applications without success. Thus, when one day he met an older schoolmate who advised him to order trinkets for resale in the city centre.

'Jeffrey do you think this will work out', Piyo asked his friend as he caressed his mineral bottle.

'Mmmmmm yaah' Jeffrey mumbled after taking another bit of the seasoned chicken slice piece.

'You can give it a try for two months and come back to me', Jeffrey assured his friend his searching eyes gazing at him.

Piyo shied away nodding his head good-naturedly more out of acknowledging his friend's encouragement.

As they enjoyed their food at this Chicken Inn outlet Piyo listened attentively to Jeffrey's sojourn to Dubai as he recounted the several trips that he had taken to secure orders for bales of clothing, and different types of trinkets. There was the hustling to secure visa and last-minute air tickets purchases and flight bookings. Dubai to most people in African countries had become the gateway to the Middle East countries. The big business people were now into trading in fuel from some oil producing countries.

Piyo had listened to his friend imagining how great it would be to one day seize the opportunity to fly out to Dubai. But today he had to contend with his lateness.

Piyo jumped into a high roof commuter omnibus just a few moments before it took off at this popular intersection of the neighbourhood location. As the speeding commuter bus headed towards the bridge, Piyo raised his eyes to get a better view of the landing airline. No, this was not the Emirates Airlines he had thought but the South African Airways preparing to land on the runway. Each time they passed adjacent to the runaway a piece of his mind always reflected on the Dubai story.

Fumbling his pockets, he felt for his torn purse. For a fraction of a second his heart lept with panic, but he relaxed moments later. In haste he had thrown the purse inside the paperback that he now held on his lap. That he now remembered. So from the very purse he now pulled out a dirty United States one dollar note and forwarded it to the conductor. Patiently he waited for his change.

Not long there were in bustling and hustling of the city. Wriggling his way through the mass of human traffic he gritted his teeth with anger at the obstructing people all driven to the city by the quest to survive. Shoulders brushed roughly on each other, others stamped on each other's feet rushing their apologies in the confusing movements.

On the intersection, the traffic officer summoning all bags of tricks fought hard to control the traffic jungle.

Piyo's mouth went agape. He had been late and today his selling post was already occupied. Stamping his feet in anger he waited agonizingly for the late arrival of Mr. Patel from where he had left his trinkets the previous day. Around him tongue lashing voices could be heard echoing and competing all in an effort to win customers. Individualism had gripped young men, women and the elderly all in an effort to survive

'The Cult of the Hustle' all centred on going on it alone, being your own boss had addicted all the populace for through encouragement right from the family, church and community everybody felt being an entrepreneur in his or her right. Piyo found himself in the thick of this dog eat dog affair.

'Municipal police!', a piercing voice shouted from nowhere. That voice was enough to alert all. Suddenly the street vendors took to their heels in different directions. Amid the fleeing trinkets and fruits were strewn in the tarmac as vendors escape in different directions in an effort to avoid arrest. This time they had been smart, though some of their trinkets and fruits were strewn all over the tarmac others had quickly hidden in bale shops. The battle had been briefly won, Municipal truck swept past loaded with heavily armed men wilding rubber baton sticks.

From a street corner Piyo stared his heartbeat pounding heavily. His last fear was being jailed. No, he did not like to take any further chances. He had one idea in mind, to return back home.

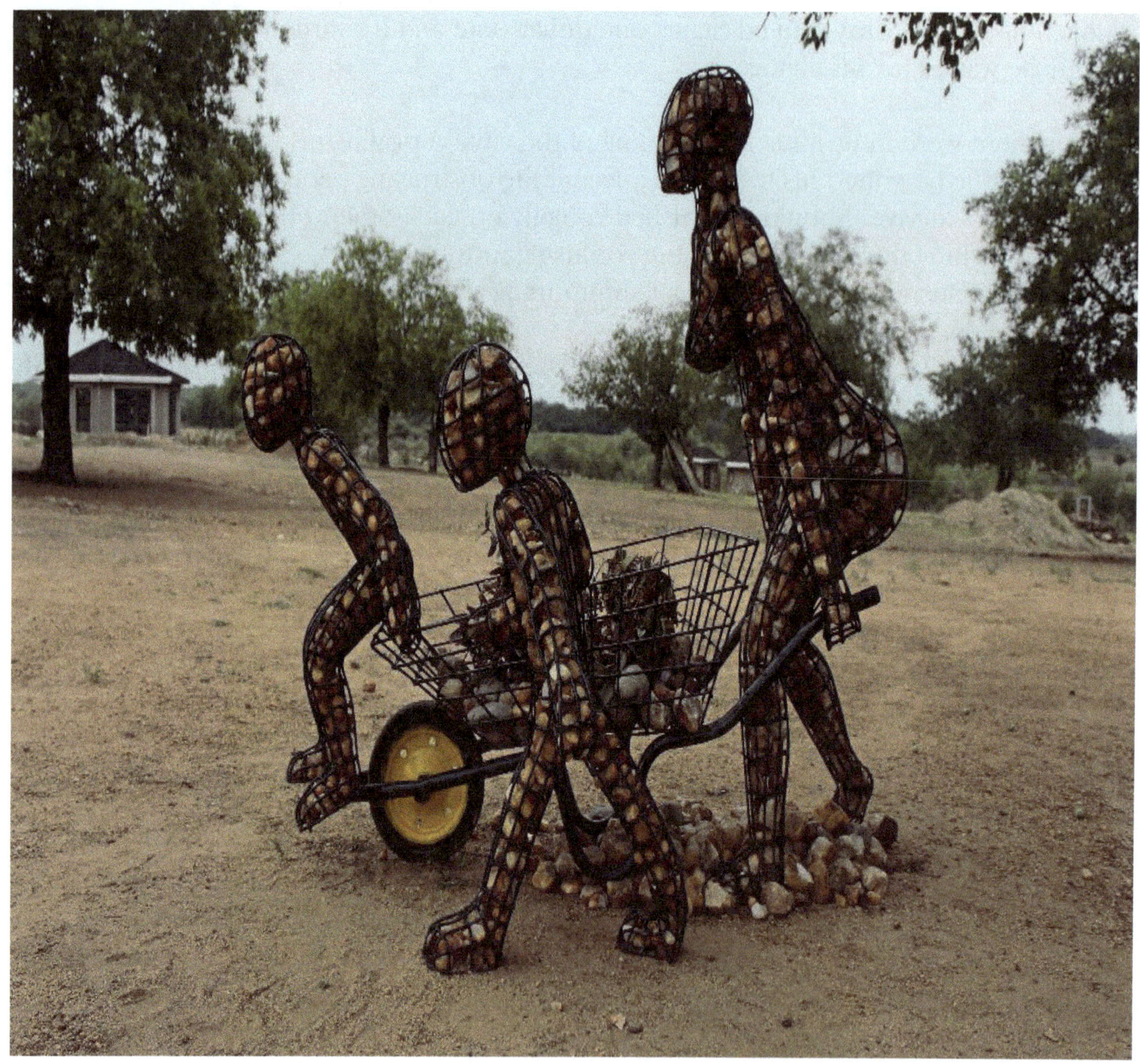

The Mother and her sons

Boniface Matemba

It is a sculpture of the mother with her sons playing with her whilst she works the field. These Mother's sculptures are a celebration of mothers who carry light above their heads so everyone could see and also running household and being a part of family

Pains of a Widowed bride

Tanea Nyika

As the dawn of 18 November broke, with a few sun's rays streaming in through my rusted windows casting a soft glow across my room, I suddenly regretted being born. There I was sitting alone, just as how I came into this world, alone, in my favorite rocking armchair, moving but going nowhere. Alone, as I'd been my whole life and my mind racing with the same pace of the chair but still, just like the chair, going nowhere.

Deep inside I've always had that haunting sadness, my mind, a tumultuous sea of memories and emotions, each wave crashing against the shores of my consciousness, leaving behind fragments of pain and regret. Deep down I'd always known that the devil will catch on to me and that thought could never allow me to settle or hope for any better future. The weight of my sorrows always seemed to hang in the air, suffocating me with its heaviness but that morning as I gazed out the window at the gentle, golden hues of the sunrise, I knew that I was about to live the events of the day that would shatter my world. The day the devil would finally get his claims. Again and again I tried to escape the reality of this wedding with what I'd known of him but the dilemma as always, had me on it's horns. I vividly recall the day all my respect, love and admiration for him came falling down just as how the diamond pieces of the other necklace he'd bought me had also fallen down after he stripped it away from my neck with all his might for simply denying him one night.

The day is still etched in my memory with unforgiving clarity, a day that had left me heartbroken and adrift in a sea of despair, the day that had left me in this desolate moment of solitude and sorrow on a day that was supposed to make me the merriest, a day I'd forever planned and rearranged as a girl. All dreams were shuttered by the truth that the devil for once allowed me to see that early morning as I was on my usual morning jog. As a passed by my fiance's house, the young, affluent Mayor named Byron, I decided to stop by and retrieve my puppy that the nanny had been looking after for me the previous day. I noticed the main door standing ajar and, receiving no response to my calls, I decided to enter the house.

After a while of yelling 'Pitzy, Pitzy', I heard what I assumed was a bit of moaning coming from the slightly ajar bedroom door. Assuming it was Pitzy, I ventured into the room assuming that Byron was on his work trip as he'd said. The room was filled with utter darkness and slowly, I opened the door like the mechanism of a spring loaded gun afraid that Pitzy might sneak out before I noticed. Blindly, I searched on the walls for a bulb switch for the light. As soon as the lights were on, I met the utter horror of all horrors in my life. On the bed was a naked brunette and my fiance. Caught between anger, pain, and a lingering love for the man that stood before me, I started shivering uncontrollably as the cold chill slowly swept over my spine. Finally some words found their way out of my throat. "I need time," I remember I'd said in a slight whisper as my eyes searched his for any sign of sincerity. "Time to understand, time to heal, time to decide." I'd added. The silence in the room was so deafening, broken only by the sound of my own racing heartbeat and a distant crack of the bed as he went back to sitting down. There and then I knew I wasn't going to be granted any time as I'd bravely said but rather, it was the time for unending threats and bribes to promise that I wouldn't shame him and indeed that afternoon the threats began the same way he'd done to get me agreeing to marry him.

Indeed the shock of the scene had left me paralyzed and unable to comprehend the devastation that had unfolded before my eyes. The man I was about to vow my life to, had shattered my trust and broken my heart in the cruelest of ways. As I stumbled out of the house that day, the weight of betrayal and disbelief clung to me like a heavy cloak, and the world around me blurred as tears stung my eyes then freely breaking into two thin streams down my cheeks, just like that, on the 18th of November as I waited for the cars to start arriving. As soon as they did, I ran to the bathing room. I allowed myself a good sip in the bathtub as the warm water blended with my tears. The weight of the day ahead was already bearing down on me. The sound of laughter and chatter from the arriving guests filtered through the walls, a stark contrast to the turmoil within my heart, even now. Each moment of joy and celebration would be a cruel reminder of the pain and uncertainty that now defined my love story. With the knowledge that I'd to go in front of people and look strong I let out the last sobs with a depth of emotion that threatened to consume me. The echoes of my cries filled the room, a symphony of grief and longing for the love and trust I had once believed in. The once bright vision of my wedding day then felt like a distant dream, replaced by the harsh reality of a fractured heart and a future shrouded in doubt.

Wiping away my tears, the resolve in my eyes cut through the despair. Standing up, I looked at myself in the mirror, a silent promise forming in my heart. The day indeed had started with tears, but I tried to refuse to let it end in defeat which was in all ways inevitable. Then again I reasoned with myself as to why I'd chosen to wed in November, a month highly known for misfortunes but well November or no November, one's character wouldn't change. With a deep breath, I gathered my strength to step out of the bathroom but couldn't. I wasn't ready to face the day and the uncertain future that lay beyond it. The sound of the approaching celebration grew louder, but within me, a quiet strength began to take hold, a flicker of resilience amidst the storm. As the gentle but persistent knocking on the bathroom door continued, a flurry of activity unfolded outside. His sisters were so eager to support and the makeup artists, determined to make me look my best. A lot of exchanges cheerfully went on and compliments about the grandeur of my impending marriage to the mayor. Yet, within the cocoon of my thoughts, I grappled with the weight of my inner turmoil.

With each step toward the chair and each brush of makeup against my skin, I felt the weight of their well-intentioned words. The facade of privilege and prestige that surrounded my impending marriage to the mayor felt suffocating, a gilded cage that threatened to confine my spirit. The whispers of envy and admiration from the dressers only served to deepen the chasm between the reality I faced and the illusion of happiness that the world saw. As I looked at my reflection in the mirror, the weight of expectations and appearances went down on me more and more. The knots in my stomach tightened with each passing moment, my heart heavy with the knowledge that my so-called "luck" came at a steep price. The words of congratulations and admiration rang hollow in my ears, even now they still do, a stark contrast to the ache of uncertainty and fear that defined my reality. In the midst of the whirlwind of preparations, a quiet resolve managed to take root within me. Beneath the layers of makeup and the opulent gown, I still carried the burden of a truth that could not be concealed. Despite the facade of privilege and admiration, I knew that my journey ahead was fraught with challenges and sacrifices that no amount of grandeur could mask.

Stepping out of the car, the grandeur of the cathedral and the overwhelming festivities enveloped me in a wave of sound and color. The jubilant cacophony of car horns, ululations, and laughter filled the air, a testament to the spectacle that the wedding had become. Multitudes from all walks of life had gathered, their eyes alight with curiosity and excitement, eager to witness the union of two prominent figures. Amidst the sea of faces, the groom stood at the altar, resplendent in his immaculate tuxedo, a picture of confidence and anticipation. As I made my entrance, I was so grateful for the veil which concealed a torrent of tears as the crowd murmured in hushed admiration of my prison, probably mistaking my emotions for the expected display of sentimentality on such a momentous occasion.

Beneath the veil, my tears flowed unchecked, a silent testament to the tumult of emotions that threatened to consume me now and again. The weight of expectation and obligation hung heavy on my shoulders, the grandeur of the cathedral a stark reminder of the suffocating opulence that had come to define my existence. All that while, I longed to shatter the illusion of joy and celebration, to scream out the truth that lay concealed beneath the layers of tradition and spectacle. I wish I'd betrayed him just as in the days of Hitler when those little kids spilled all the truth about their parents, I wish I had.

Walking down the aisle, the weight of my tears mingled with the weight of the ornate gown. The world around me saw a bride immersed in the emotion of the moment, but within me, a storm raged, a tempest of defiance and resignation, a silent scream for freedom and authenticity. As I reached the altar, Byron's eyes met mine, a mask of joy and expectation veiling the truth that lay between us. In the stillness of the cathedral, amidst the opulence and grandeur, I stood at the precipice of a life-altering decision, but could only give out tears, a silent plea for understanding and liberation.

Stopping in my tracks, the world around me seemed to blur, the weight of the moment amplified by the unexpected sight of my ex. The badge displayed prominently on his chest, identifying him as a member of the Mayor's security team, which added a surreal layer of complexity to an already tumultuous situation. In that singular moment, the past and the present collided, and the truth I'd sought to bury surged to the surface. The presence of my ex, then entwined with the grandeur of the cathedral and the prominence of the occasion, felt like a cruel twist of fate, a reminder of the tangled web of connections and obligations that bound me.

As our eyes met, a myriad of unspoken emotions swirled between us, a silent exchange that transcended the weight of the present moment. Byron, unaware of the charged atmosphere that lingered in the air, stood beside me, his gaze filled with anticipation and joy. Yet, in the depths of my heart, a maelstrom of conflicted emotions threatened to engulf me and if it be possible, even choke me to death. As the cathedral stood to witness the grandeur and tradition of the occasion, I stood at the crossroads of my destiny. As the wedding ceremony reached the pivotal moment of exchanging rings, a hushed anticipation filled the cathedral. All eyes being fixed on us, immersed in the solemnity of the occasion. However, amidst the reverent silence, a figure walked purposefully down the aisle, his imposing presence unnoticed in the midst of the congregation's focus on the groom and I.

Heavily built and bearing a steely resolve in his expression, the intruder moved with a singular determination, a silent force that disrupts the veneer of celebration and tradition. Unnoticed by the assembled guests, his presence stood as a stark contrast to the grandeur and opulence.

In the midst of the charged atmosphere, the figure reached the altar, his presence was such a disruptive force that cast a shadow over the ceremony. The weight of his unspoken intentions loomed large. The unexpected arrival of the enigmatic figure became a harbinger of uncertainty, a disruption that pierced through the facade of the celebrations In the stillness of the moment, a silent question hung in the air, threatening to shatter the illusion of joy and unity that the wedding sought to embody. Just then I noticed the same badge as he pulled down his face mask. The sudden and jarring sight of the intruder brandishing a pistol, his intent unmistakable as he targeted the mayor, sent shock waves of panic and disbelief through the cathedral. In an instant, the solemnity of the occasion gave away to a scene of chaos and fear. "You won't get to abuse that power, son." The words hung right under the expected sound of the bullet that hit straight through Byron's chest. Falling to the ground with him in my arms all I could see was the blood which was oozing profusely onto my gown.

The gasps and cries of the gathered guests filled the air in that harrowing moment, a cacophony of alarm and confusion reverberating through the once serene space. Turning to my right, I saw my ex still seated as he was when I walked in with a smirk on his once handsome face. I wished that I could rip him apart but he'd given back a small piece of revenge and I knew there was definitely more.

The Zebra

Boniface Matemba

The Zebra sculpture is a commemoration of thousands of Zebras that grace Kruger National Park during the summer time. They move along in herds, eating grass as they travel from one camp to the next. This zebra is made up of steel sheets and round bars. It incorporates

lines and sheets to highlight the distinct colors of the zebras

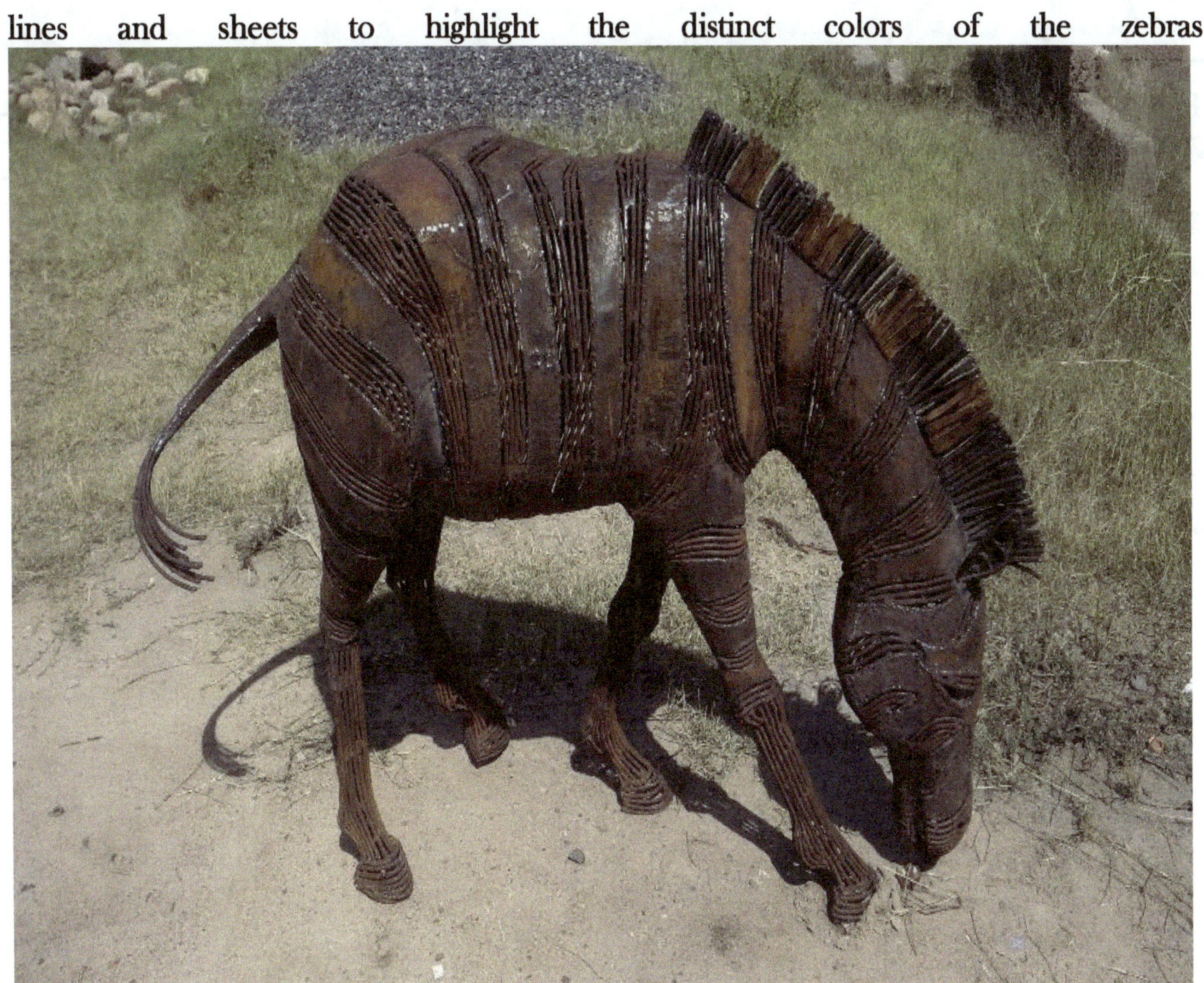

Pieces of Wood

Matthew K Chikono

The foot tall maize plants were turning yellow in the scorching sun and I knew by the end of the week we were going to lose the entire crop; it meant another year of getting by. Not once had it rained the entire month of November.

I wiped sweat from my forehead with the back of my hand. Weeding was exhausting, worse whilst choking on the dust raised by hoes hitting the dry earth. The burning sensation of an empty stomach reminded me that I could faint if I didn't take a break. Beside me, my grandfather wiped his nose. He didn't seemed to sweat but I knew he was struggling as much as I was. He was in his mid-seventies and that kind of work was now decades behind him.

I stood up for a moment to stretch my back. My eyes glided across the one acre field we were farming. It was surrounded by many others of the same size belonging to our fellow Chisi villagers. However, it was the only one with maize, a crop not suitable in our particular region. My grandfather noticed me eyeing our pending doom.

"Don't worry Tigere," he said," It will work, we have done exactly what Hubert Carlos did at his farm."

Hubert Carlos was a white farmer my grandfather had worked for in the seventies. My grandfather claimed that the farmer had grown maize in a more hot and arid condition than we had in Chisi. My grandfather had convinced me to follow this farmer's method and plant maize for that season, he was sure it would succeed. It now seemed the promised bumper harvest would not suffice.

My grandfather continued tilling the ground. His voice, between the heavy breathing, started narrating all the marvelous and miraculous farming that white man had done. He continued telling me about his own life and work at the farm. My grandfather recalled and narrated his younger days when his life seemed hard. It made his less sad. I let him tell the story again.

We decided to take a break from the weeding. It was almost noon and we had to eat our lunch. We sat under the trees at the edge of the field and started eating mangai; a boiled salted seed mixture of maize, groundnuts and cowpeas. We shared a bottle of maheu which we sipped to make the food swallow easily.

After our lunch was done we continued with the weeding. From the corner of my eyes I could see the old man panting. He was exhausted.

"You should go home and rest now Sekuru," I offered, "I can manage alone."

"No Tigere." The man wheezed, "I am still capable."

I didn't insist, afraid to wound his already fragile pride. He didn't want to be seen as a declining old man. He kept pace with me until my own back started to hurt. Fortunately, we finished the entire field a couple of hours before sundown. We did not linger to admire our handwork, but went straight home.

We didn't have any cattle that needed to be herded home from the communal grazing lands at the end of the day. It made him sad, my grandfather, that he was now an old man without a single cow to his name. Neither a single goat nor a rooster to call his own. Each and every year he had relied on miracles to survive on the little that he harvest on his field. The little money I made from doing odd jobs in other people's fields bought cooking oil and salt in the house.

What he had was a home. Acres of farmland surrounding three thatched huts. The effects of time were visible on the walls of muddy huts. What used to be a chicken run was now a single waist level wall. The blair toilet stood proud on the leeway side. A pit was all that was left of the kraal that used to snuggle in a dozen or so cattle he owned during his prime. The three dilapidated huts, a toilet and a well was all he had now.

It was in one of the huts that we went in, kicked our sandals off, and put our feet up in the air just for a little while before we started preparing supper. I took some dried wood outside and put on a fire inside the kitchen. In a minute the whole hut was filled with smoke. I dashed outside in order to catch a breath of fresh air and bumped into a body.

"Good evening Tigere," the man said, "Is Sekuru Jemusi around?"

The mentioning of his name made my grandfather spring to his feet and rush to the door to see who was looking for him. There was a look of contempt on his face when he realised it was our neighbor, Zuze, who was asking about him. My grandfather hated Zuze, he claimed Zuze conspired with other witches in the village and killed his first wife.

"Good evening Sekuru Jemusi," Zuze said, "There's a donor at our church giving out food parcels to the elderly next Tuesday. Send Tigere with your ID card to register. I have already registered myself and now I am telling all my fellow neighbours to do the same."

Zuze didn't wait for my grandfather to reply. He started walking slowly towards his own homestead. Zuze loved his neighbor, enough to tell him about food parcels despite knowing fully that the neighbour hated him. My grandfather was sure that his stance at a local missionary church was a rouse to distract people from finding out how deep he was into witchcraft.

I watched Zuze walk away, he was as old as my grandfather. If my grandfather's accusations were true, then I owed my existence to that man. Without him killing my grandfather's first wife, my grandfather would have never married Marujata who bore my father.

My grandfather went back into the kitchen and sat on the stone bench. I followed him and sat beside the fire, stirring my pot.

"I have been reduced to this," the man started," my enemies feel pity for me, that they help me to find alms from strangers. How did my life come to this?"

I didn't have to answer. I didn't even look in his direction, I couldn't bear to see tears on his face. The man had five children with his first wife none who had visited him in over a decade. His second wife had borne him two sons neither had left home. The eldest, who was my father, comfortably rested in the family burial grounds whilst the younger son was somewhere in the village getting drunk to whatever he could lay his hands upon.

"Promise me Tigere," the old man sobbed," that you will bury me when I am dead. Promise me you will only abandon me after death. You are the last of my family you know that right?"

I continued stirring the pot murmuring something about him rumbling nonsense and needing rest. I thought I heard the old man cry but I couldn't make myself look. Later, I dished him sadza and dried kapenta.

"We are not eating together Tigere?"

"No grandfather," I replied, "I am going to the well to fetch some drinking water and I will eat when I come back."

I took a quick glance at the old man, he was struggling to chew with the few remaining teeth in his mouth. I slipped into the evening, leaving the empty bucket behind.

I took brisk steps towards the Msasa tree which stood tall and proud near the cattle dip tank. I found the two sisters waiting patiently. The younger sister started slowly walking away as soon as she saw me approaching.

"Why does your sister hate me that much?" I asked the older sister.

"I told you Tigere," Eustancia said,"Lukia is extremely shy."

Eustancia gave me a quick hug whilst her sister was looking away before breathing in my ear,"I missed you."

"How will she be able to bear it when I marry you and become her brother-in-law?" I asked.

"You shouldn't joke about marriage like that Tigere."

"I am serious," I said, "I want to marry you Eustancia."

"Then marry me tomorrow Tigere," Eustancia continued, "If you can't afford it, my aunt can help me elope in the evening."

I left her words hanging in the night air. The moon was slowly rising and a handful of stars were already tingling in the sky. Eustancia and I had been in love for a couple of months but I hadn't noticed how she was such in a hurry to get married to me.

"Listen Eustancia," I said, "you are still eighteen, there is no need to rush."

I went on explaining to her that before I could take her to my home I had to make a little money to support the family we were going to have. At that moment, I was struggling caring for my grandfather. I promised her only a couple of months were needed for me to go to the city and work it out.

"How are you going to find work in Harare?" She asked.

"I have been in contact with my aunt, my father's half-sister, she said I could live with her whilst I sort it out."

"What about your grandfather?" Eustancia asked, "who will take care of him during the time you are gone?"

I didn't answer, I didn't know the answer. My mind went back to earlier that evening when the old man had made me promise him not to leave him until his death. Odd how my future depended on the promise I didn't make.

"Lukia let's go home," Eustancia finally said, "Goodbye Tigere, we should get going if we ever want to reach home before midnight."

"My fault, I came late today," I said grabbing her hand, "my grandfather was talking a lot about his life, I couldn't leave him talking to himself."

"Your grandfather tells you a lot about his life," Eustancia said, "maybe you should write a book about him and call it leaflets of life or something."

I chuckled. One day, when we had started seeing each other, I had told Eustancia I wanted to be a writer. I was impressed that she had remembered that. Maybe she was the one. Why did she desperately wanted to be with me that much? It didn't seem like she was in love with me or something.

"Bye Tigere," she said, letting go of me and holding her sister's hand at the same time walking away, "remember I won't wait for you forever."

I wished she had kissed me, it would have made her sister uncomfortable. Also it would have made me happy. Wasn't it what love was supposed to be? I started walking back home. Unbridled thoughts of raging my twenty three year old brain, not sure what my life was supposed to be.

I reached my grandfather's homestead. The fire from the kitchen wasn't visible from the outside and I thought that it had gone out. I picked up some dry logs and twigs and went inside. There was some still red charcoals on the fire place. I put on the twigs, blew on it, and the fire quickly ignited.

The illuminating fire showed my grandfather still sitting on the stone bench slumping weirdly on the wall, his unfinished plate of food on the floor.

"Why are you sitting in the dark grandfather?" I asked him.

The silence told me the answer I wasn't ready for. I didn't have to touch him to know what death felt like, I could smell it in the air. I stared at my grandfather, hoping to catch a glimpse of death who had taken him away from me.

The Charging Hippo

Boniface Matemba

Hippos are known to open the mouths widely and exert loud ferocious grunts so as to intimidate and assert dominance. It is made of round bars. It has different lines to highlight different details of a hippo

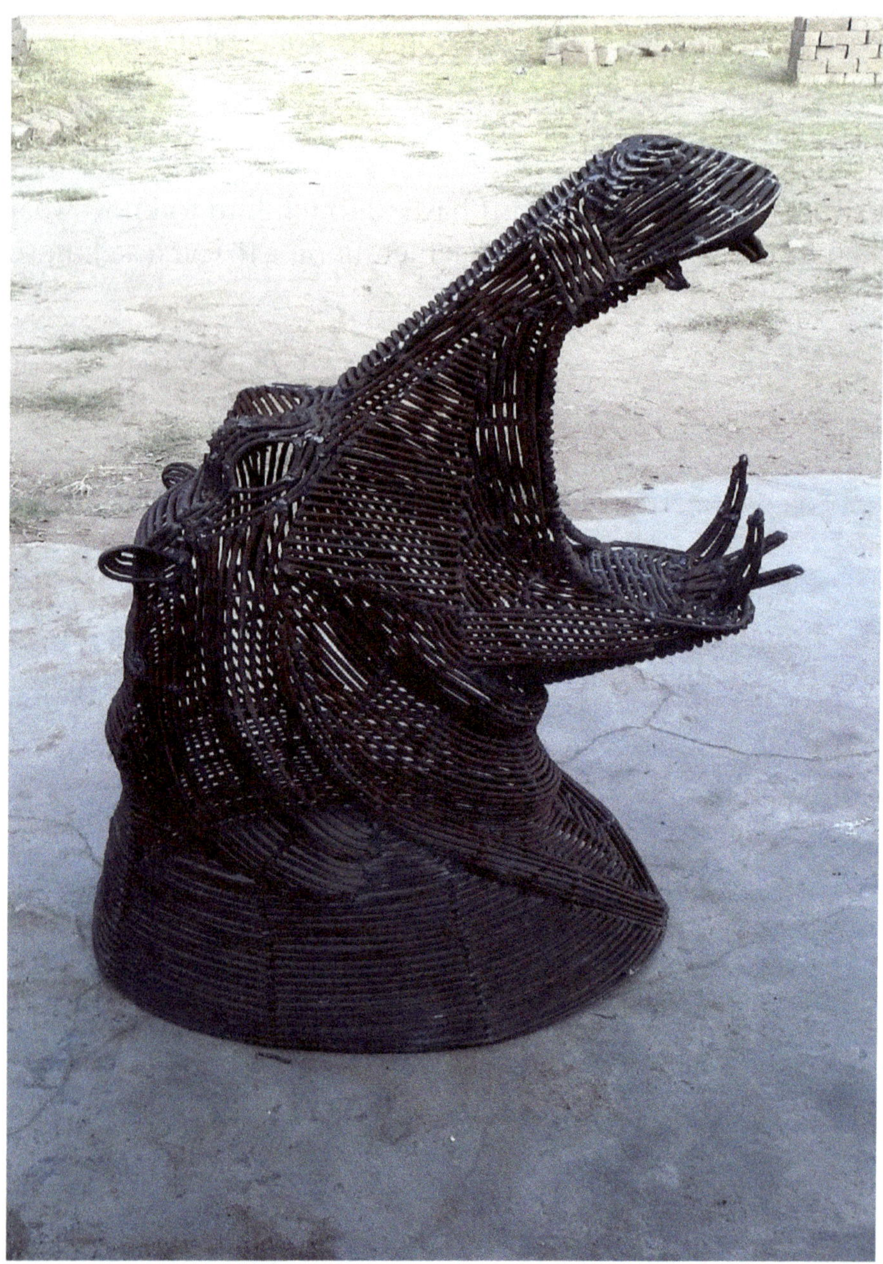

THE LAST PARTY

Placidia Chiwita

I have never been a fan of parties. I can count the number of parties I attended in my life with a single hand. I can't exactly say what I dislike about parties. Maybe it's the crowds, or the loud music, maybe it's the forced socialisation with people I hardly know.

"We used to be troublemakers at school," Tanaka was saying at the front. "Every time there was noise and the back, the teachers knew that it was us."

I am at a party and the loud girl making a speech is my old friend. This party is different, I know everyone here. This is a party thrown specifically for me. Everyone gathered here today left their homes and came here for me. I feel kind of overwhelmed but happy, very happy.

Tanaka is still speaking and I laugh at what she is saying. It's all true. We really used to be close back in primary school. Ours was a classic enemies turned to friend's situation. She came in as a transfer student when we were in Grade 5. One look at her and I could tell she wasn't your typical transfer student, the ones who are meek and quiet, who slink silently into the background while observing to see where they would fit in. No, Tanaka was loud. A day in and she already had a band of followers. I envied her for that.

I was always quiet in school which is why I don't remember what happened for us to clash and almost fight. Quiet as I was, I still never backed away from a fight. We would have gotten in trouble if we had fought inside the school premises, so we made an appointment to fight outside the gate after school in a typical primary school student's way. When school finished, I made my way out in my lonesome and sure enough, Tanaka and her band of followers were waiting for me outside.

Needless to say, the fight never happened and Tanaka and I became as thick as thieves since then. To make it even better, we were put in the same class for our Form 1. My family moved away end of that year and I lost contact with her. Over the years, I saw her maybe three times when I visited my old neighbourhood. Last I heard, she had moved overseas, which is why I was pleasantly surprised to see her at this party.

I feel a hand on my shoulder. I turn around and see Mrs Moyo, my very first boss. Come to think of it, I have never had a male boss in my life. She started that chain.

"It's good to see you baby," she says, pulling me into a hug.

She always called me baby even when I worked for her. It made it easy for me to call her mum, especially considering all her children are older than me. She looks good, though she has gained a lot of weight since I last saw her years ago. She used to be very strict about her weight, I guess not anymore. Seeing her like this, I realise I missed her.

"How is the family?" I ask.

She throws her head back and laughs, "Growing. Munashe now has 4 kids!"

"What?"

"I know!" she says.

Munashe is only a few months older than me, how does he have four kids and I have none? Wait a minute.

"With the same mother?" I ask.

"Three different mothers," she says with a shake of her head. That explains a lot, he always was a womaniser, he even tried his luck with me.

I still haven't forgotten the $500 she borrowed from me when business was low and she never returned it. I never struck up the nerve to ask and I am not about to do it now, her presence means so much more.

I spot my mother going around and interacting with the guests. Melody is with her. Sweet Melody. We became friends at university and after all these years, we are still tight. I had more friends back in varsity and when we graduated, we kept in touch for a while and then with time, as we took different career paths and some got married, the communication ceased. I understand distance often puts a strain on relationships but I don't understand friendships that end when one gets married. Girls are even advised to distance themselves from their single friends when they get married. I still understand the reason for that. Perhaps they thing that us single girls will corrupt the married ones. It's different with Kudzi, her marriage didn't affect our friendship at all.

Speaking of Kudzi, I hear her contagious laugh. She is huddled at the back with Nyasha. Whatever they are watching on that phone seems to be so funny, I can see Nyasha's shoulders begin to shake. I wonder if she still has that habit. Back at school, we all knew to stay out of Nyasha's arm reach whenever something funny was going on because she would hit you. Some habits are hard to drop so I observe and wait. Soon enough Nyasha's hand comes up and she hits Kudzi's shoulder.

Hard.

I crack up in laughter and the two of them look at me, Kudzi rubbing her shoulder and Nyasha wiping the tears of glee from her eyes. Those two girls, we became friends in 'A' level. We were a band of six and we used to sit at the corner of the class. We had so much fun back at school, just remembering those days makes me smile. From the sleepovers where we would spend the whole night watching Korean dramas instead of studying, to the prayer sessions at the school grounds. Those girls made my school days memorable. I lost touch with most of them as time passed, except Kudzi. She stuck around even when life landed us in different countries, even when she got married and had children naming me Godmother to her son. I can't believe I have known them for over 20 years. All six of the girls are here and my heart is almost bursting with joy.

Oh, there is Mr Marange, my Form 5 and 6 class teacher. Look at that white hair! I am glad to see he still looks fit. I remember when he saw me the first time as I was applying for 'A' level, he told me to study economics because I would be good at it. I didn't listen and instead favoured geography. I have since regretted that decision and my stubbornness. 'A' level geography kicked my ass people, it did me so bad! It did everyone bad but especially me! Imagine having two As and an E! Instead of the 14-15 'A' level points I was aiming for, I ended up with 11 points just because of geography. All my hopes to get sponsorships went down the drain. To make matters worse, economics had such a high pass rate, everyone I know had an A in economics. I mean even Rudo got a B and it was common knowledge that she wasn't the brightest in class. If only I had listened to Mr Marange, I would have gotten my 15 points.

Wait a minute, is that? Yes, it is. I ignore the pain and run to him.

"Sir!" I say as soon as I reach him. He gives me a bright smile and pulls me for a hug.

"Good to see you kiddo!" he says. Mr Nhau, my old Shona teacher at 'O' level. He is one of the people I always wanted to see before I die. I never saw him again ever since the time I collected my 'O' level results many years ago. Until now! I am happy I got a chance to see him. Our relationship had a rocky start. I don't know how I moved from being his most notorious student to being his best one. In his defence, maybe it was because my notoriety wasn't that bad. I mean, it was just a simple case of late-coming. I was always late to school and he was always on gate duty. The number of punishments I had to do because of this man. He ended up accepting that I will never be early for school and my lateness became a subject of laughter. Soon enough, he was looking out for me and sometimes even waited to hear how I found the exam he had set for us. He would never admit it but I know I was his favourite student.

Behind him is another former teacher of mine, Mr Murwira, and he is holding a copy of Sidney Sheldon's Doomsday Conspiracy. He used to teach at the school where I did my 'A' level. He didn't directly teach me, but we always clashed because of my late-coming. This late-coming habit started from way back, I don't know what happens, I wake up early to start preparing but still end up late. Anyway, we discovered our mutual love for reading one day as he was supervising our punishment and since then, he started lending me books to read. He had a Sidney Sheldon collection and that was the time I fell in love with that author's work, may his soul rest in peace.

"I have known Rufaro for the longest time," a male voice was saying. Now who could that be? I don't recognise that fat man standing at the front. I walk closer and .... Hell no! What is Tawanda doing here and who invited him? I look around and see my mother giggling into her hands. Of course, it was her, she is the only one who would find this funny.

"We were so tight back at a school," he was saying scratching his belly.

Make him stop.

"I thought we were going to get married..."

Can someone please get him off that stage!

Only my parents and my 'O' Level school mates find this funny. The rest of my guests are looking at him with a mixture of mingled curiosity and confusion. He used to be so handsome back at school, and I had a huge crush on him. Almost everyone knew that, then he had to go and break my heart by dating my friend. I remember that I locked myself in my room and cried for days. Where is the betrayer? Not here? Good. She knew I liked him and went ahead and dated him. She was clearly not loyal. I have no use for backstabbers in what remains of my life.

Looking at him now, I wonder what I found attractive about him. He isn't wearing his age well. Those red eyes, big belly, oh boy Tawanda has lost the plot, and his looks. I can tell underneath of that flesh and filth, there is a handsome man waiting to come out, if he just takes better care of himself and stop smoking whatever substance is reddening his eyes and blackening his lips.

Oh well. I almost feel sorry for him then I remember the reason everyone is gathered here, then I feel sorry for myself.

And is that...?

"It's good to see you Rufaro," he says.

OMG! What? How? When? Damn can my heart stop beating so fast? I should probably close my mouth too. He pulls me into a hug and he smells so divine. How did he grow from a scrawny little boy who was the smallest in the whole class, to this? He grew into his looks that's for sure. If I had known he would grow up to be this hot, I wouldn't have rejected him all those years ago. We would probably be married with a bunch of good-looking kids by now.

In my defence, I don't have the gift of foresight, I mean he literally reached up to my chest and was so bone thin back in high school. Now he is easily the tallest man here, that body shows he is good friends with the gym and that skin is showing that he has a good skin care routine. And that beard! Damn that well-trimmed beard looks so good on him. I wish I could turn back time, I even forget that I am dying for a minute.

"Close your mouth, a fly might just fly in," Laura whispers in my ear. I immediately close my mouth and swallow.

"When did you become so hot?" I ask. He looks shocked at my directness, then bursts out laughing, Laura giggling behind me. I suppose this is the moment when normal people would feel ashamed, not me. Shame has no space in my life at this juncture. I see a ring on his finger. So, he is married. It's a good thing he didn't bring his wife. I don't want to see the woman occupying what could have been my position.

"I agree, Roy you are serving the looks," Laura agrees.

"It's nice to see that you two haven't changed after all these years," he says with a chuckle. "And it's really good to see you again Rufaro," he says, pulling me into a hug and walks away. I turn to Laura with a mournful look on my face.

She laughs and pulls me into a hug, "Shh, it's okay to cry," she says. "It's okay to mourn for the love that could have been but never was because you lacked the foresight to see a hunk that was hiding behind that skinny boy. I understand friend."

I fake crying on her shoulder and that invites another fit of giggles from her. Laura was my high school friend and classmate. We got close because of our mutual love for Korean dramas, reading and writing. We kept in touch all through 'A' Level and reconnected when we went to the same university. We were tight for the first two years, then she became distant. My texts went unanswered, promises broken and calls unanswered. On a call that she did manage to pick up, I vented to her on how the friendship was one sided and it seemed like I was the one chasing after her. After that, I stopped.

She must have lost my number, or deleted it because I later heard she was looking for my number from a mutual friend. He didn't give it to her. It would be years later, when I had a lot of airtime that was almost expiring and no one to call, that I scrolled through my contacts and came across her name and called her. She was so happy! I could hear the joy in her voice on that call and she chastised me on having her number and not getting in touch at all those years. We kept in touch since then.

"And look who else is here," she says. "If it isn't your first real boyfriend."

I look and yes, it is him. Oh Chris. He looks good and he wears glasses now! I have good taste on men if I do say so myself. I smile as I stare at him, we might have broken up ages ago before we graduated but we had some good times. He was my first kiss too. What makes him so memorable is that he is the only guy who sat me down and told me exactly why we couldn't continue dating. I cried my eyes out and hated him for some time.

It was after continuously meeting men who chose to treat me like trash and go quiet on me instead of ending the relationship that I got to appreciate Chris. Ladies, a man who sits you down and talks to you about ending a relationship is noble! Appreciate him. Men these days extend a lot of energy in pursuing you but when they are done, they would rather treat you bad in hopes that you get the hint and end the relationship first, or else they just ghost you as if they aren't the ones who were blowing up your phone when they wanted you.

Oh, and there is Jeff! He flew all the way from Canada for this? I am so touched and I think I'm going to cry but I can't do that because all these people who are here for me and trying to be strong will cry too. I met Jeff at a summer program many years ago. We didn't meet again since that program ended, until now. What is he holding? He starts waving it at me and it's a miniature version of a rollercoaster ride. I throw my head back and laugh. This is so like him! We went to an amusement park during the program and I somehow ended up teamed with him. We went around the park trying out all sorts of rollercoaster rides, screaming like banshees on some of them, very dizzy on most and feeling exhilarated and wanting more after all of them. That was my first encounter with adrenaline rush and I loved it. That is a memory I kept close because I never went back to an amusement park since.

Oh, there is Hope and Hillary, the very first women to mentor me. Hope was my career mentor while Hillary was my spiritual mentor. These two women made a significant impact in my life and I will always be grateful to them. Hillary always cried easily and it's no surprise seeing her cry as she talks about my growth.

My parents come and sit on either side of me. I put my head on my father's shoulder and hold my mother's hand as I listen to Hillary speak. My parents made this possible, they came together with my friends and organised this amazing party for me. I don't know how they managed it, but they invited everyone who was important to me. How they managed to remember everyone, I have no idea.

Everyone gathered here today was in my life for a season. These are the people who brought a smile to my face whenever I thought of them. Some of them left after that season had passed while others stuck around. I look around and spot Kudzi and Melody sitting at the back. They had become close friends because of their mutual friendship with me and it has been a joy to see.

What makes me happy is that everyone here knows the reason they are gathered here, they know I am dying, they know that this might as well be the last time they are seeing me alive but none of them are crying. They are looking at me with genuine joy at seeing me again, they are standing on that stage and speaking about what a good person I am and the impact I have had in their lives. They are bringing up long buried memories and thanking me for things I had long forgotten. Some of them even dug up old photographs that I had forgotten and I got to laugh as I went through them.

Instead of writing statuses and long social media posts after I am gone and not able to see it, they are telling me their words now when I'm able to hear and appreciate them. They are saying goodbye to me while they still can. As much as I am in pain right now, and it hurts so bad, I am just happy that my illness managed to prepare my loved ones for my inevitable demise, it gave them a chance to say goodbye.

Death is no stranger to any of us. We don't often think of it, it's the one thing we all know is coming but we tend to ignore. In the times that we do think of it, we want it to be the quick, it has to be painless. Dying peacefully while sleeping is everyone's dream. I know it was mine.

The reasons for this are mostly selfish. No one wants a painful death. A visit to the hospital leaves most depressed. And then we tell ourselves it's because we don't want our loved ones to suffer. They will be plagued with hospital bills if I get sick for a prolonged period of time we say. I don't want them to see me waste away in pain we think.

But perhaps an illness, as much as it hurts, will prepare those remaining behind and give them closure. As much as we would prefer a sudden death, it tends to come as a shock to our loved ones and makes it difficult for them to accept and cope.

I have watched my parents and friends go through the five stages of grief. Denial when I was first diagnosed with Stage 4 stomach cancer.

"No, it can't be! There has to be a mistake. How come we never saw it?" they said.

Anger as they saw the cancer eat away at me. The pain, the retching, not being able to keep anything down.

"Why is this happening to you? Why is God letting this happen to my daughter? Why her?" they said.

Then came the bargaining, begging the doctors please save me, begging God to heal me, attending all night prayers, fasting and climbing mountains.

Depression when they saw no change, as I continued to get more and more frail, as the cancer spread and the times where I had to be rushed to the hospital in the middle of the night because of the amount of pain I was in.

And finally, acceptance that their little girl was on her way out, that they weren't going to spend Christmas with her. They made a decision to make my final days as comfortable as possible and also make the best of what little time they had with me.

I worry about them, how are they going to cope when I'm gone? I always told them to have more children but they kept insisting that I was enough. If I had siblings, I wouldn't have to worry so much about their well-being after I'm gone. Now they are going to be left alone. Had I not been so career oriented, I might have settled down and given them grandchildren. That way they would always have a part of me even after I am gone.

When death is calling, it puts a lot of things into perspective. You start rewinding your life like a cassette and thinking what you could have done better and I will tell you now as someone who is going through it. What I regret the most are the birthdays I missed, the harsh words I once uttered, the time I wasted pursuing meaningless things, the times when my pride prevented me from contacting my loved ones, the relationships I let go of and the places I didn't get to visit. It's not the money I think of these days or the job but the relationships, because at the end of the day, the people in your life are what matters.

I am grateful that I got a chance to reconnect with most of them before I die. Looking at them gathered here, eating, dancing and laughing brings me joy. They will probably cry at my funeral but now, right now all I see are people who are happy to see me.

This is indeed the best funeral anyone have ever gotten. It is the best party I have ever attended; it is also my last party.

The Peering Hippo

Boniface Matemba

This shows the peering hippos of Kruger National Park which float in the water and reveal half of their heads to the surface. It is made of round bars

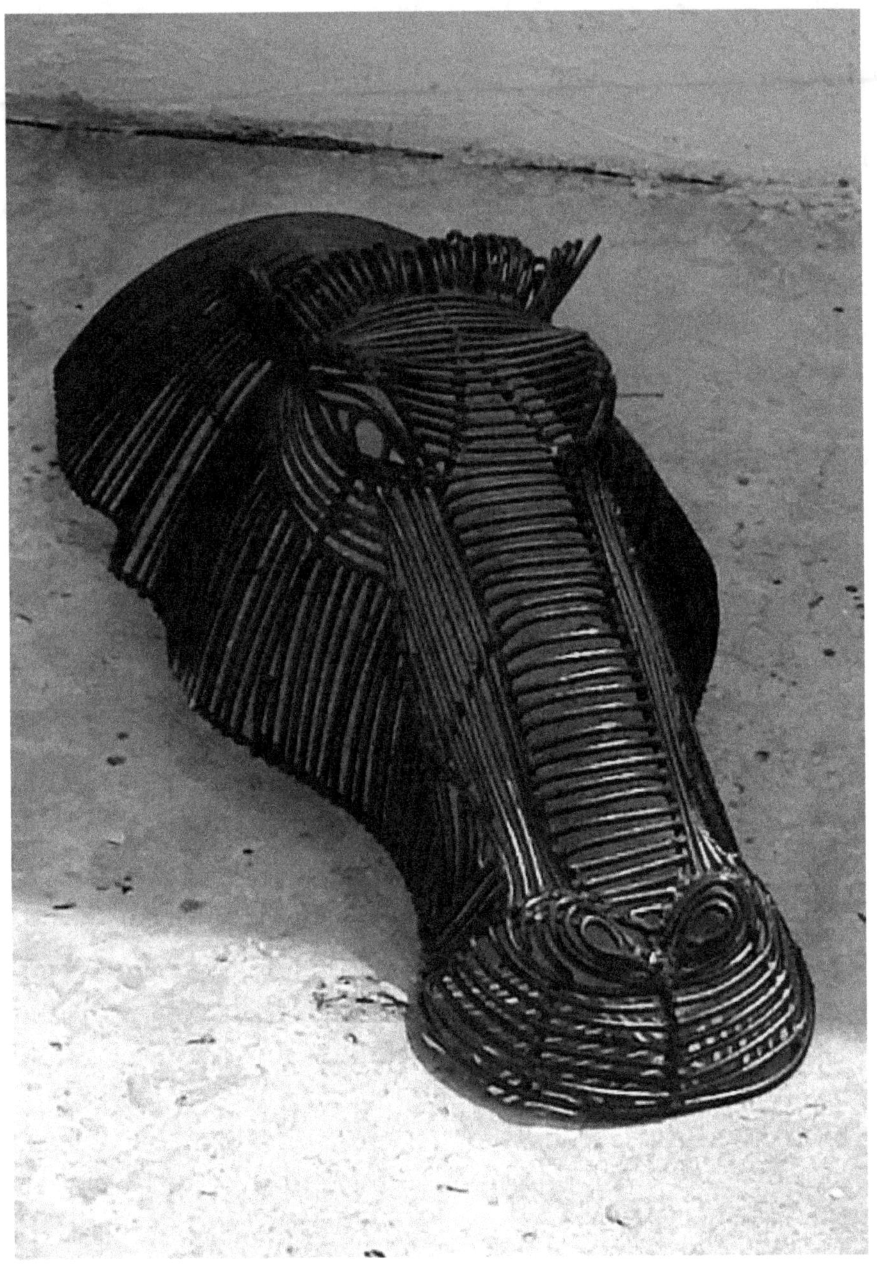

The Dust is the Theory

Tendai Rinos Mwanaka

We were full of beef, always looking for attention, behaving like utter freaks. My closest friend who wasn't a close relative was David Mukonomushava. I heard he died a few years ago. Growing old is becoming a witness on how everything you have valued starts disappearing until you wonder, is this all you were ever meant to do in life. Being a witness, but who would witness you if you overstayed everyonė, when death was exhausted of death, who would console you? Of course I was much more close to my cousin, Fungai, whom I shared the same class with from Grade six onwards, we also sat on the same benches in form 1 and 2. With David we were inseparable for some time, at the height of my hunt for mischief. Every Friday we always stayed behind doing punishment for infractions we had incurred during the week. We were anti-establishment to the hilt. If the school introduces any rule which was an infraction to our independence and freedom, we would fight it head on. There is a time the school introduced English speaking to improve English understanding, they said. I think Mr. Chibvuri was behind it, as he was the acting head waiting for our substantial headmaster, Mr Nyamandwe, who was on leave after finishing his tenure at his previous school, St Davids Bonda, waiting to take over at Nyatate.

So they had created small stripes of papers written, "I am a Shona Speaker". Imagine the irony of having to admit to talking in your language as an infraction. Being a Shona speaker was punishable now, yet you are actually a Shona person. A drop of water had become guilty of flooding. Imagine asking an English man to be punished for being an English speaker at school. Here is what would happen, the class monitors, prefects and head boy and head girl would start with these slips of papers. They would give them to the next student they find speaking Shona. That student is supposed to give it to the next student, next student... until the last student who had those slips by Friday afternoon would be asked to stay behind for punishment and or tell the prefects who had passed the paper to them, until the whole lineage of Shona speakers that week were booked for punishment. It felt like punishing your ancestors for birthing you. And by that first Friday we had collected most of the slips and we refused to tell the prefects where we had got them. We never spoke English and we collected most of the slips and never passed them off to the next student as was the rule. It took us a few weeks to disrupt this and hoard all the slips every time they were issued, and every Friday afternoon we stayed behind doing punishment for the whole school. That was a given for us, as we broke many other rules. At one time, midyear form 2, I missed a technical drawing exam doing punishment but the teacher, who was also the headmaster, Makwaza, gave me a zero on the report card, and yet I still comfortably made the top 5 in that class. We were insufferably mischievous such that the school made sure we were never invited to any functions or events because we were sure to create drama

There is this time a local teacher died and the school closed and the whole student body went to the funeral. We were told by the headmaster, Mr Makwaza, to stay at school, afraid we will create drama at the funeral. But as long as you didn't tie us down we refused to graze where were not tied down, I am just paraphrasing the Shona proverb here, "a goat grazes around the place it is tied down on". There was no way we were going to respect any instruction. So we waited for an hour and followed the students to the residence of this teacher who had recently departed. My mother said when she saw me she hid, and when the students saw us some started laughing, giggling, gawking ... knowing we were up for it.

We started crying in high pitched voices, crying like hell had broken loose and we were squirming from the hot hell, like utter crazies, mourning this teacher. We would throw ourselves on the ground, keening and belting another glossolalia. One would have thought we were moved by this death if you were not privy to our work. We hated this teacher from our years at the primary school where the teacher taught for years of my primary school years. That teacher was a fucker of the first order. I remember how on the first day of the school, my little sister was wacked by the backhand of this teacher for messing up the school's march from Assembly. We were trained like soldiers at a barrack. You wouldn't just amble away from the assembly like the kids do nowadays. The first class, grade 1 A, then Grade 1 B, then Grade 1 C, grade 2 A, Grade 2 B, Grade 2 C....that was the system we had to follow. Not only will you be marching, stomping your feet down like a soldier, we would also be singing songs, to the drum we would mock sing to later on as saying, *gandatiganda mwana ane manyoka, gandatiganda mwana ane manyoka* would be belted, and you have to be swinging your hands twice upwards, and once downwards, your legs in synchronicity to the beat and the pace of the march as you moved in one single file from the assembly, class after class, using the alphabetical spellings of your surnames in that class. I don't think we had a surname that started with letter A in Shona, so the Bores, Binungus, Bangojena, The Chikwandingwas, Chibvuris...were up there ahead in the lines, and of course the Mwanakas were in the middle tail end of the lines.

My little sister had stumbled trying to climb the over 2 metres high steps to the grade 1 class, tumbling down taking a number of kids down with her. Only for her to tumble down again as the teacher's backhand wacked her to the ground. First day at school, a little six year old is expected to be drilled and be a perfect soldier. This teacher was a cruel disciplinarian.

And so when the head boy realized we were upto our usual tricks, a Simon Huna, who was the head boy and the other older form 4 guys grabbed us by our feet and hands, shutting our mouths and carried us off the funeral. We didn't care. We had made our point. Later, in our form 4, we lost another teacher we loved, who was my cousin, Bizzet Mapfurira. It gutted me. Even though I had performed at the primary school teacher's funeral when he died, this time I learned that loss is personal. Even though my cousin, when he was our accounting teacher, was strict on me and would beat me up if I misbehaved, his death broke something in me

He was gunned down by the police in Harare where he was finishing off his studies at Harare polytechnic, a few months after he had married his long time sweetheart. With the death of my grandmother when in form 2, I realized death stalked everything that I thought was permanent. Bit by bit loosing people I knew taught me I had to make the best out of this now. Earth was only a school, and dust was the only theory we had to learn and relearn, and relearn for a lifetime of it...

Meeting the Murewa Culture Centre based veteran international painter and sculptor, Mr Tackson Takawira Muvezwa

Oswald Kucherera.

'I was born an artist. What I do is mixed medium. I mix materials. I do not put finer details. I leave it for the imagination of the viewer.'

Mr Muveza said this as he took us on a walkabout tour of his sculptures exhibited outside his home.

As you arrive at the main gate of his home, visitors are greeted by sculptures displayed in his yard. During the walkabout tour he revealed that the sculptures used to be displayed in a personal gallery at his home. However, the gallery had since been turned into a school and the sculptures were moved onto his yard.

In the conversation he revealed to me that the chief aim of this school is to impart his skills and knowledge to the younger generation. He mentors young talented artists living in the surrounding villages. He turned his home into a centre of learning and cultural heritage. His place is well-known in the area.

When I dropped off the bus at Dandara Shopping Centre, a day before my visit to his place, I approached a random person I first met at the shops and asked for the residents of Magwenzi family, my in-laws. The person I asked responded, ' Just go up the gravel road, when you reach the place fenced and gated, strewn with 'dolls', you have arrived. They are neighbors.'

Mr Muvezwa's place, Murewa Culture Centre is unmistakable. It's strategically located along the Mutawatawa gravel road that leads to Guzha. And interestingly, Mr Muvezwa lives up to his ancestral name. His surname Muvezwa means a carpenter or sculptor.

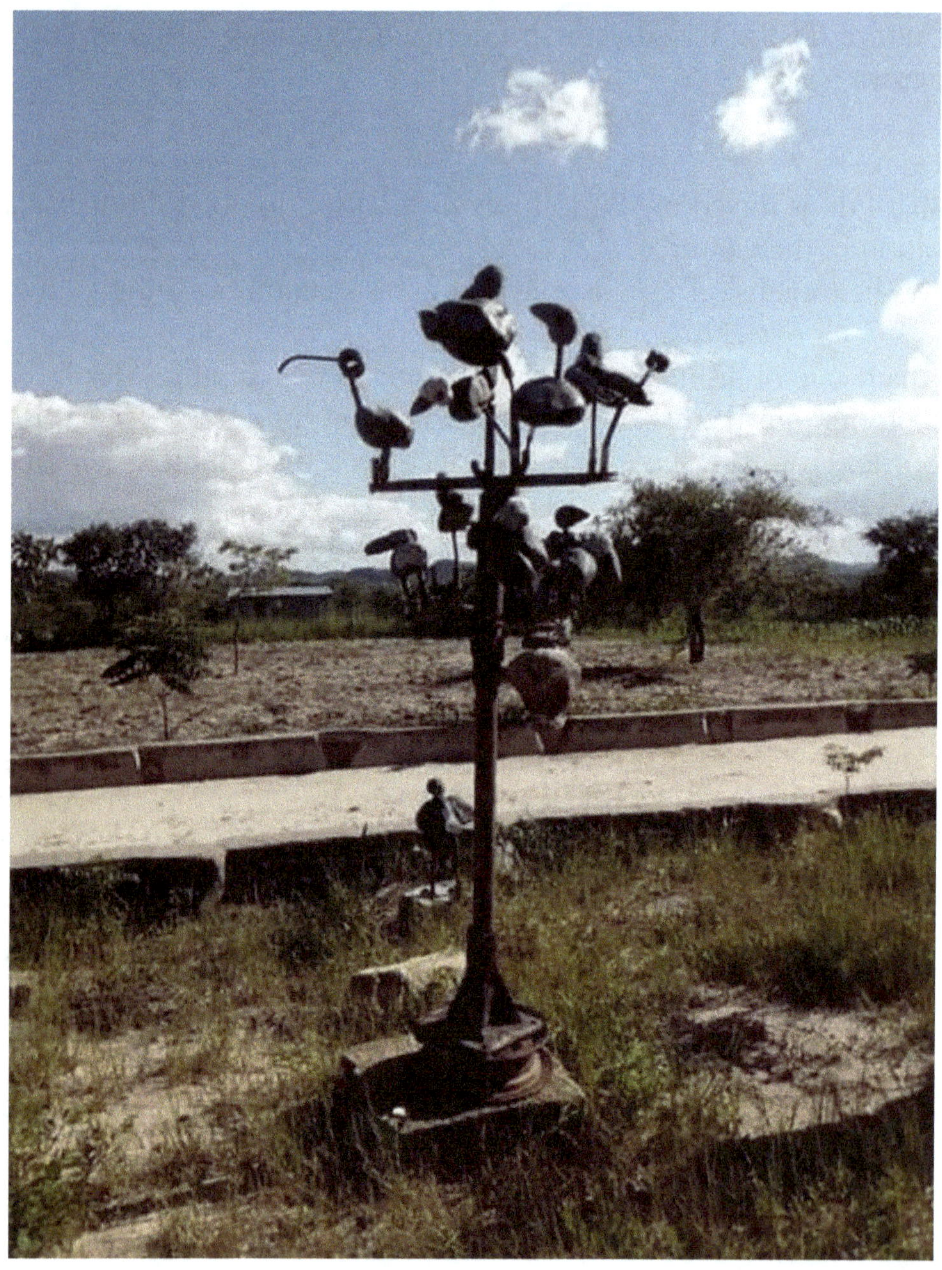

When you arrive at the gate, a writer/journalist is seen seated on a chair hitting the keyboard of an old typewriter, probably writing a story. It could be anyone. Dambudzo Marechera and Charles Bukowski come to my mind. I am immediately drawn to it. Is it a poet composing a love or protest poem, or maybe a novelist writing a novel or short story or a journalist chasing a deadline?

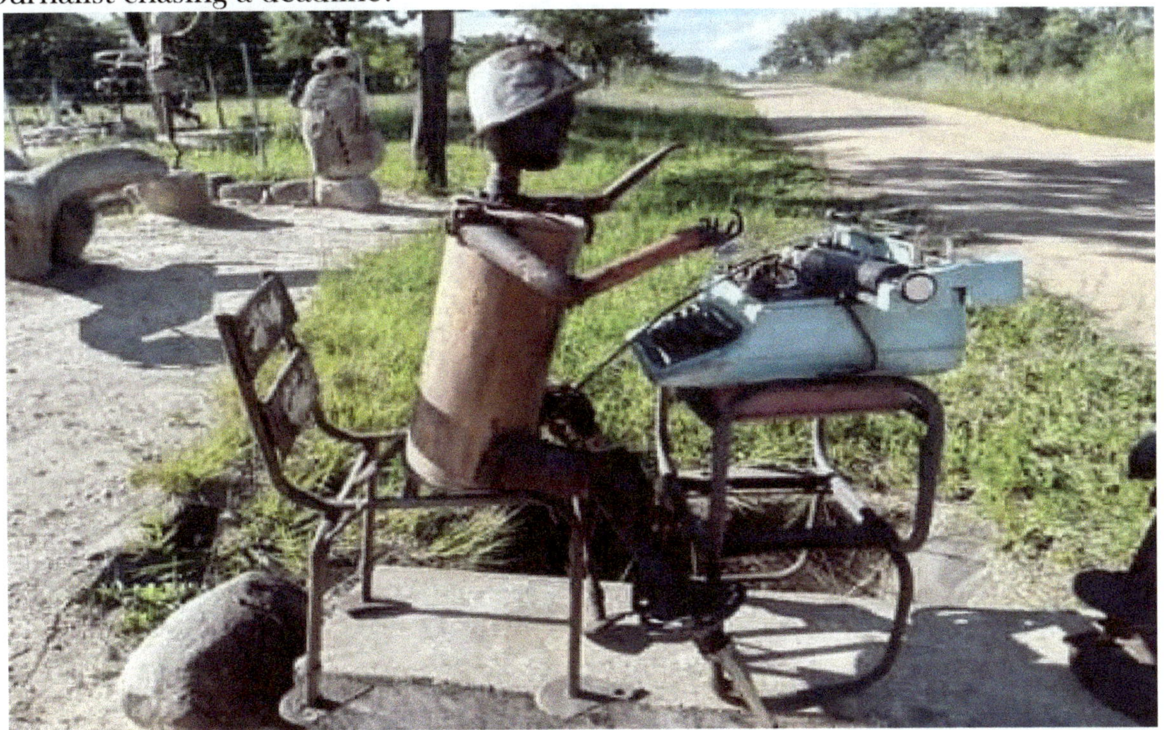

When you cast your eyes on the right side of the gate a seamstress is seated in a chair busy sewing using a Singer sewing machine. A popular and familiar brand in many households. The legs of the chair are made up of metal cut off from an old and disused bicycle. This is a very relatable sculpture. Many a household owned one of this sewing machine at one time. Our mothers or grandmother's, managed to clothe, feed and sent us to school using the money earned through sewing. My own mother had one. I have told this story a couple of times. She used to sew new or mend torn clothes, curtains, bedspreads, and many other items for sale. She has since stopped sewing because of poor eyesight.

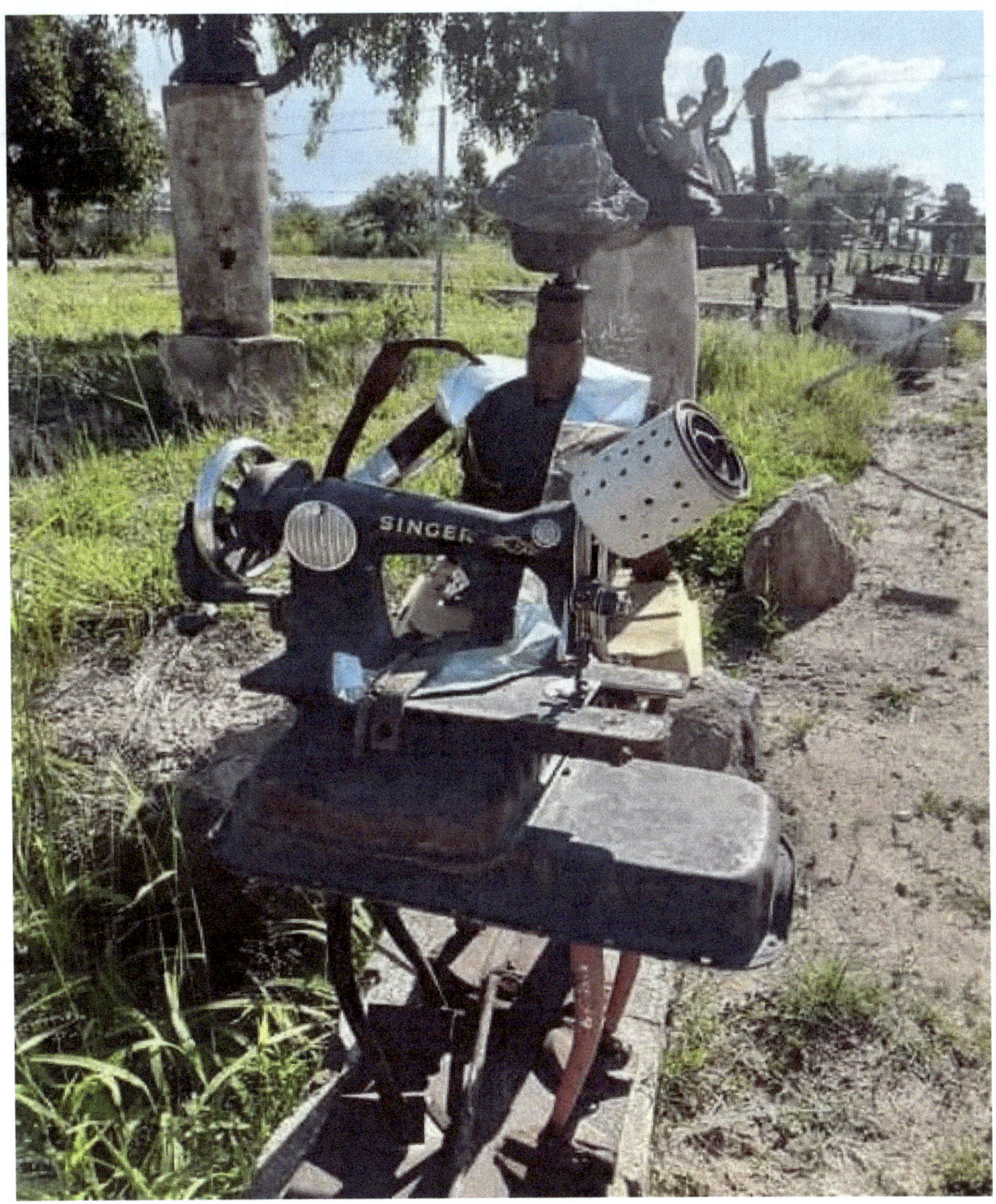
SINGER

'I worked at the National Gallery of Zimbabwe. They have my work. It's now their property though. I have exhibited my works for more than 15 years at the National Gallery of Zimbabwe since 1988. In 2012 I had a solo exhibition in Switzerland and 121 of my sculptures were showcased. But from 2013 to date I am now a full time artist based here at Murezwa Culture Centre,' he explained as we moved from one sculpture to the other.

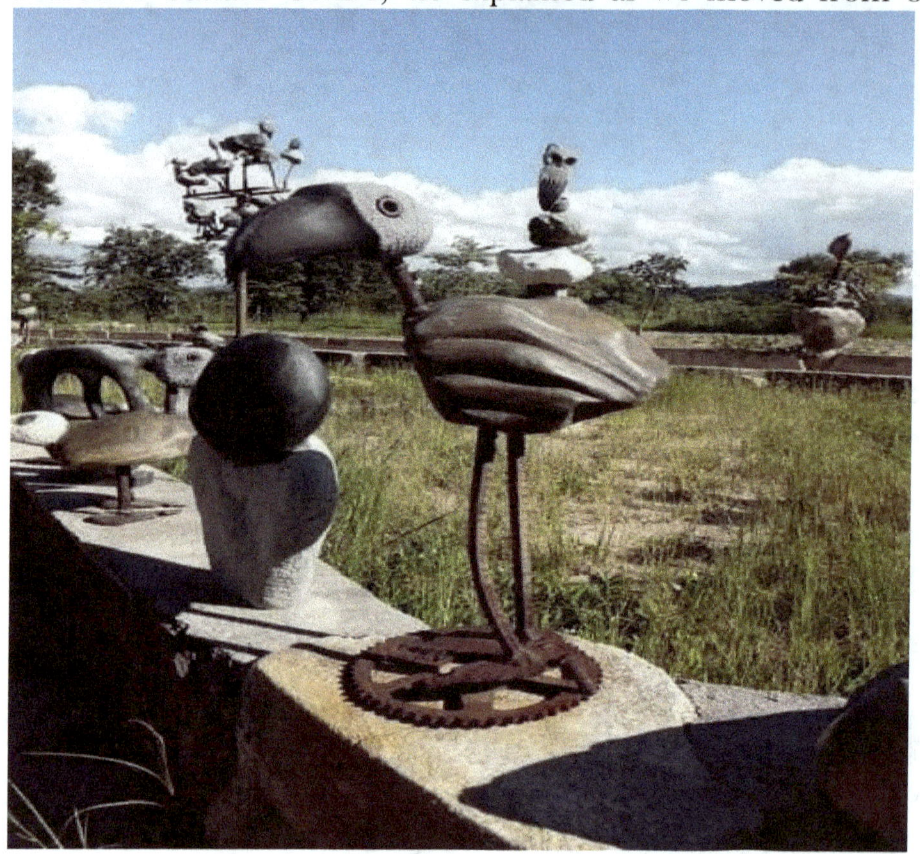

'I mostly worked with people from Holland. They loved birds. That's why there are so many bird sculptures' he continued as we toured the place.

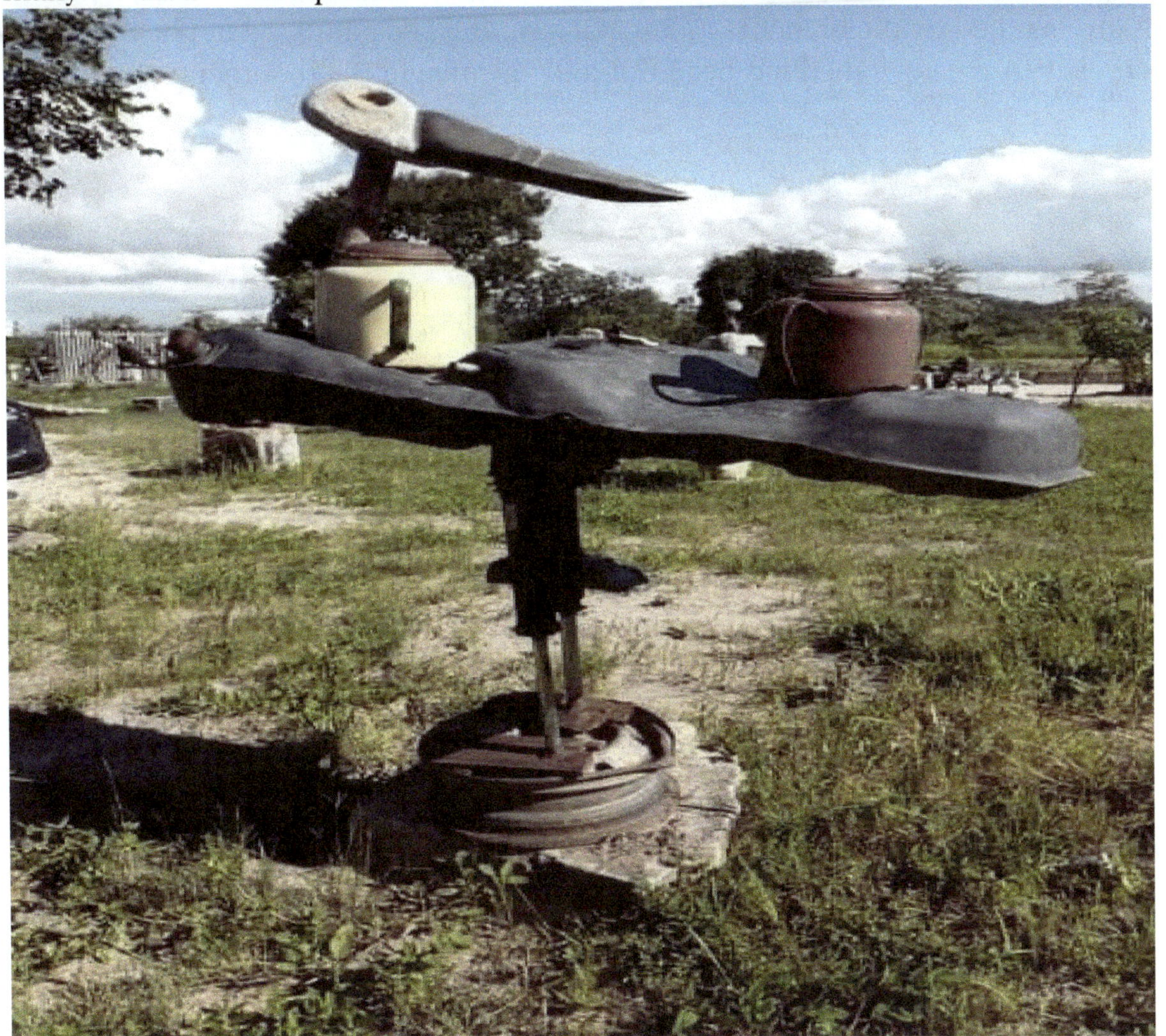

A giant bird is perched at the entrance of the gate. A string of bicycle chains are rolled together to form the body of the giant bird and a stone sculpted for its head. An old yellow car number plate placed on its chest giving it a color. Not far from the big tree at the centre of the place providing shade for people to sit on the benches erected underneath, a host of metal birds are perched on the branches of a metal tree. It's a beautiful sight. The discarded metal is recycled to create something beautiful and meaningful, and sometimes thought-

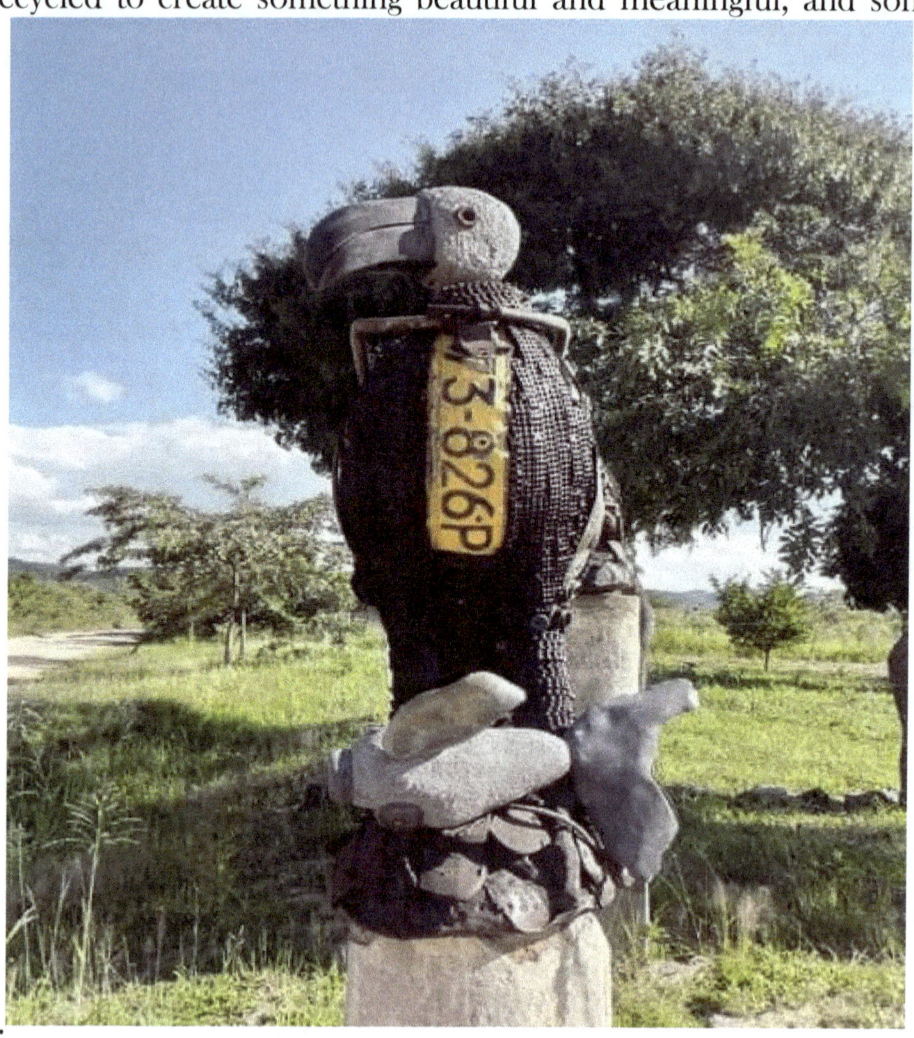

provoking.

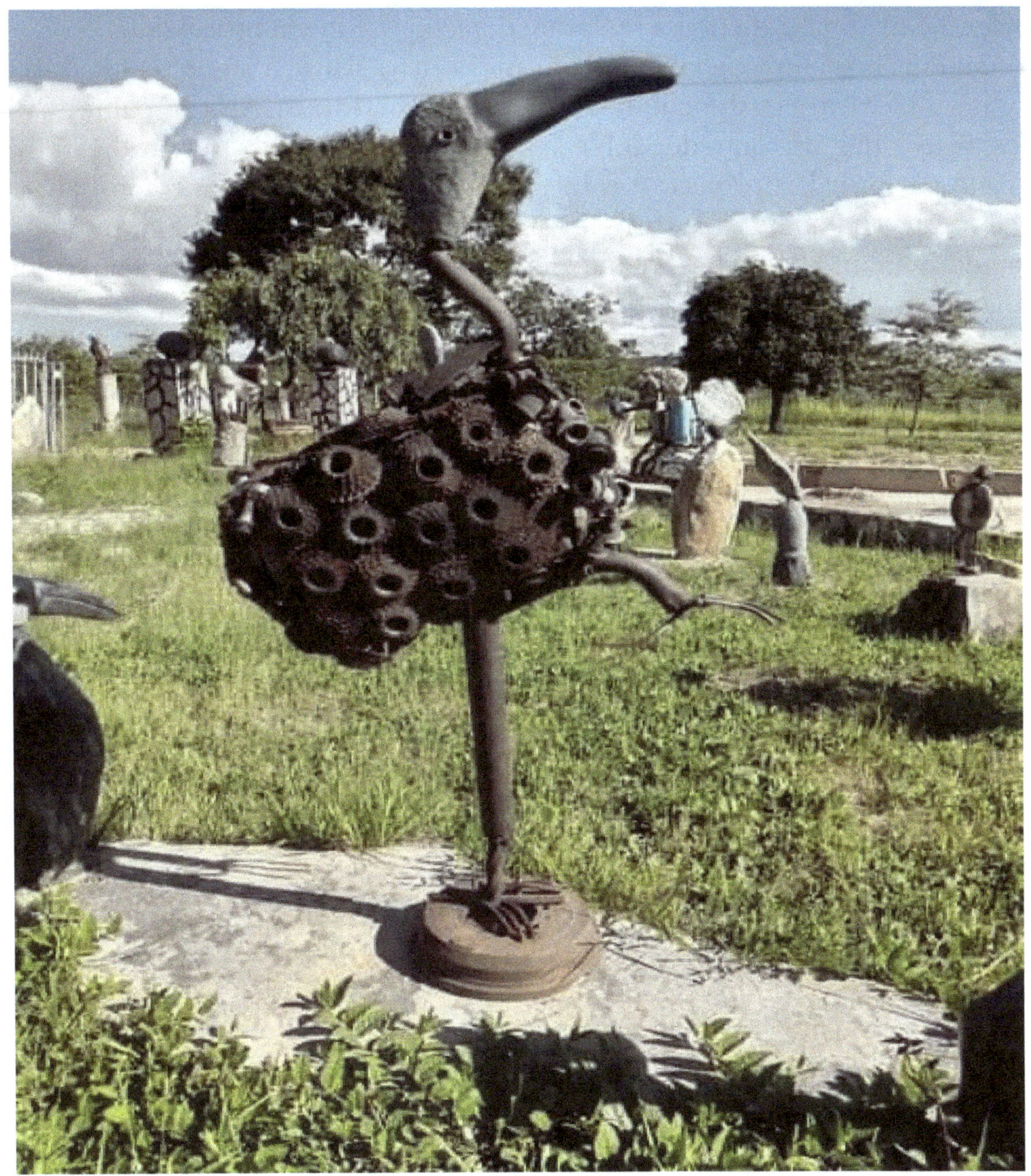

As you enter the main gate, there is a sculpture depicting a funeral procession. People are gathered around the corpse in a metal coffin, during body viewing. A stone sculpted face of a dead body is visible, lying in the coffin. In the Shona and most African cultures when someone dies, before they are buried, people are given an opportunity to view the body for the last time and pay their last respect. It is by choice though. If you're uncomfortable you are not forced to view the body. This sculpture invokes memories of death. I am reminded of my own father. It was in a coffin the last time I saw his face several years ago. The sculpture makes you think and remember those loved ones we have lost, whether very close to us or just random people we met before or never met but their stories of demise touched us. And sometimes even think of our very own impending death. It also makes you think about life. The purpose of life or dreams you might want to achieve in life before we die. The legacy we might want to leave behind for our children or families.

'I hear a lot about Cape Town. It is my hope and dream to showcase some of my work in Cape Town one day' These were Mr Muvezwa's parting words as he walked us to the gate after we had finished viewing and having a great chat with this veteran painter and sculptor.

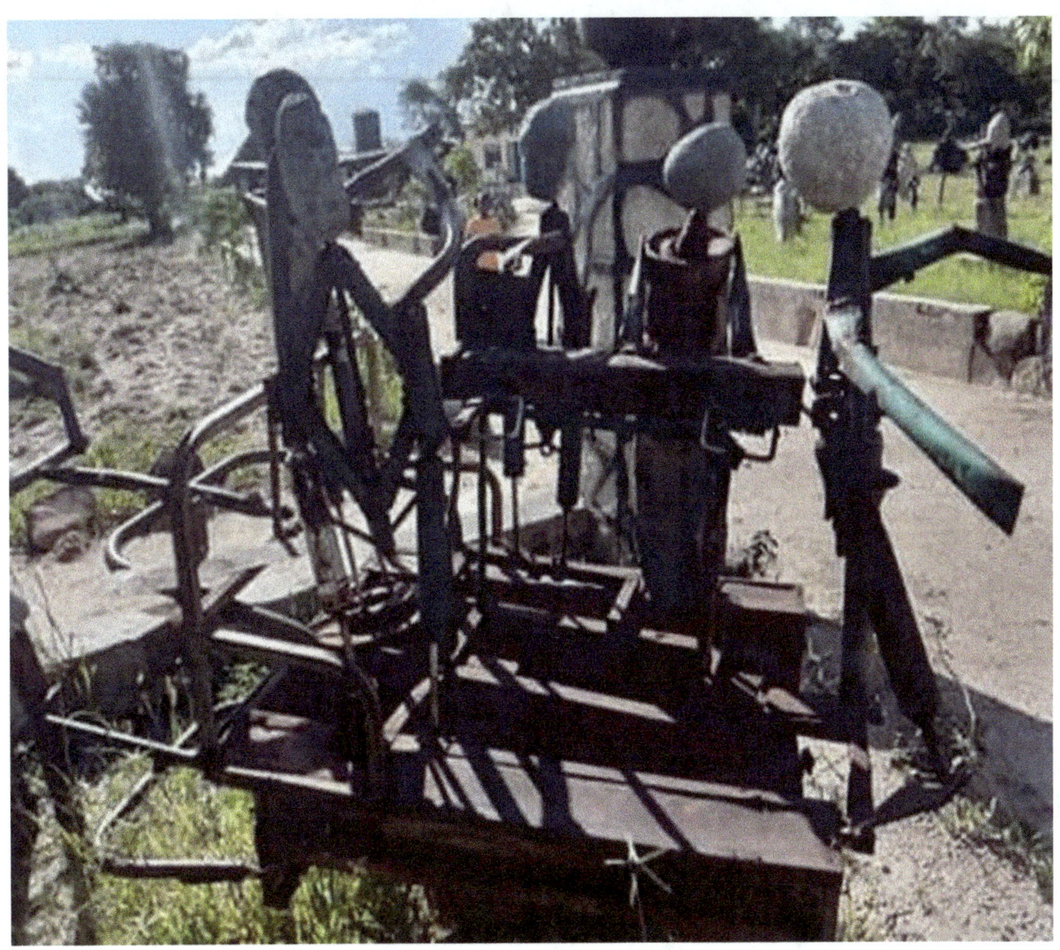

Part 2: 12 Poets and 12 Photographs

Burning hearts

Simbarashe Andrew Kashiri

And all around the fire of your heart,
In the absence of reason and thought,
Purely meditated, craved and sought,
Anything and everything to rip apart,
All of what nature in her infinite ways,
Had ordained and found suitably fit,
To endure the rest of your earthly days,
Which you dismissed with humanly wit,
Perhaps without deeper considerations,
Yet it's all normal, you're merely man,
And if ever we offered commiserations,
They would be much more than we can,
For it is by fire, that we are judged,
By fire, that complacencies are nudged.

The day's unknown king

Simbarashe Andrew Kashiri

The second drink goes down well
The day has earnestly begun.
We are all arranged here
In columns and rows clear;
Is order the necessity chaos
Wishes upon his obstinate foes?
Holding the fictitious phantom hand,
Waiting for the sigh, heave
When she yields her heavy bosom,
Onto his antique, yet original breast.
Godzilla or a city dragon seized,
The burning, lord! The searing heat!
Hell's cinders stoked- roaring flames
Kiss the night with poisoned lips
Jolts to thundering music and staggers,
Reaches for the watch to note
Time has stolen with her unforgiving stride
Mile upon mile of his timeless sleep,
Chokes back on a thirsty gulp
Knows not what measure is set
To decide who reigns upon the day...

Variegated metal sky

Simbarashe Andrew Kashiri

The sky in a variegated blue
Looks like it was dressed by the 80s,
Love songs on the radio,
Bring back time, absent minded time,
Where I look outside and see
Though without seeing anything-
It's my fight with world bureaucracy,
Maybe my plea with Geneva-
But do their even care for solitary
Dreams nearly half a decade old?
I've read and re-read the truth,
My story, the story of 3 million,
Who though in the universe's grace
Are yet to meet her gentler face...
Pain is pain and like love is fleeting,
Fleeting, fleeting memories of life-
But they don't have love here-
The city bleeds with violence and guns,
Incinerators cloud the air with abortions,
The rich gloat, the powerful oppress-
(Which one of these seven hells?!
My mind screams in its muffled state.)
The metal sky is clouding over,
A puffy somberness for ritual and tradition-
I've seen omens, felt my own ESP-

When my mind by circumstance tweaked-
Into life things that time can't explain-
I continue to age and wait,
I'm a believer so it's mind over matter,
Somber thick rain clouds variegated-
With splashes of black and white and gray,
Float away, gradually to reveal
An amazing, brilliant transcendent sun...

Liquid girl

Simbarashe Andrew Kashiri

Midnight only car engine tainted
Vivaldi's piece fills the night air.
Homing beacon, the blinking star
Whose falling light tentatively envelopes
Her face, her laugh lines spidery
Around the eyes and her full lips.
Missing your voice and addictive touch,
The brush of our skin on mine-
Butterfly kisses, that ferocious heat
When you open your mouth to mine.
Unable to sleep once again dear,
Without your warm breath on my face,
Your fingers on my restful arm...
The smell of your sex my love
When you just left the bathroom,
Your name entwined with mine,
The heart beats as one tragic tone,
Deaf to the shaking walls,
Sound aftershock when another car leaves.
Mural of the soul, when you smile,
And ignite a longing for my unknown.
There is a tiny sparkle in your eye,
I guess you miss it when it's mirrored,
There is a potion in your ways,
I drink it with eternal lust;

Spit out the seeds to grow myself
A forest of mosaic liquid girls.

Seasons
Simbarashe Andrew Kashiri

In my mind's steady eye,
I see myself, and a friend
Trying to roast a discovered bird,
Over the glowing embers of a fire.
Him saying his father's cook,
So he also knows how to cook.
I remember powder-blue, spotted-eggs
We salvaged from their grassy nests,
And when the grown ups in terror,
Breaking-voice, near hysteria ordered us
Inside the house as they murdered
A determined king cobra in our backyard...
The opaque waters of irrigation gulleys
That once filled our stomachs
As we, for the umpteenth time,
Disobeyed orders not to swim therein.
It's all coming back to me,
Dad, strangely exclaiming to mom,
"The writer has died!"
And I, all of fours years old,
Wondering what death meant.

Now I am grown up I know,
And I know there is no escape...

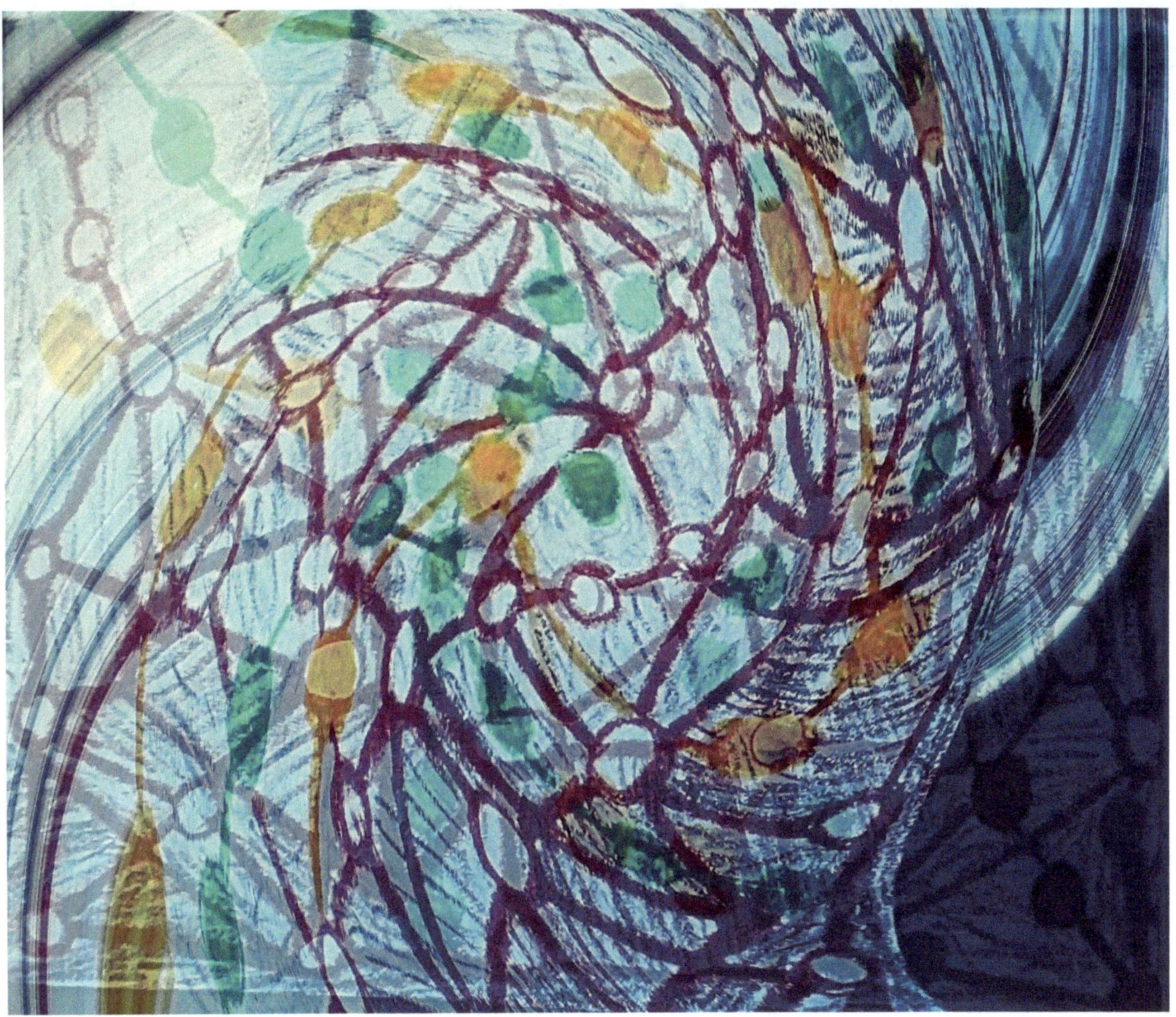

Distortion and swirls
Tendai Rinos Mwanaka

He is going out tonight
Tinashe Muchuri

End of the road.
Come and be my first.

One dream

Tinashe Muchuri

One dream takes you to your destiny
One nightmare takes you to your big fall
Remember to walk up to your destiny
Remember to wake up after the big fall
Remember to spread your wings after reaching your destiny
Remember to gather yourself after the big fall
and become a big rise.

Chasing after butterfly in the garden

Tinashe Muchuri

The soil's rainy soaked beauty presents us with new roles
The butterfly and I in the garden
It is an intended tour of the flowers in the garden
Ours is not a Garden of Eden
I am not Adam and the butterfly an EVE
God has not instructed me not to eat fruits from the tree
That one in the middle of the garden
There is no tree in this garden, but flowers and the flying butterfly
with yellow dots on black I am chasing after
It flies towards the marigold flower, the one our neighbour gave to mother
I am moving towards it and it rotates around the flower
What attracts this butterfly to this marigold flower? I ask myself.
Is it the yellow dots on its wings? Is it.....
It flies down to the Flame Lily, with red and yellow blooming flower
My sister brought from the wild thicket
I chase after it
Sliding on the clay-loam dark soil
The butterfly seems to love the chase
I looked down, on its shadow
It appear as a small airplane touring the mountains, and the vegetation
The beds in the garden look like small hills over which the airplane passes over
in its tour of the universe
Our shadows are all colourless
The flowers' shadows are colourless
We are colourless in our pursuit of beauty
that appear to us in colours and mixed colours

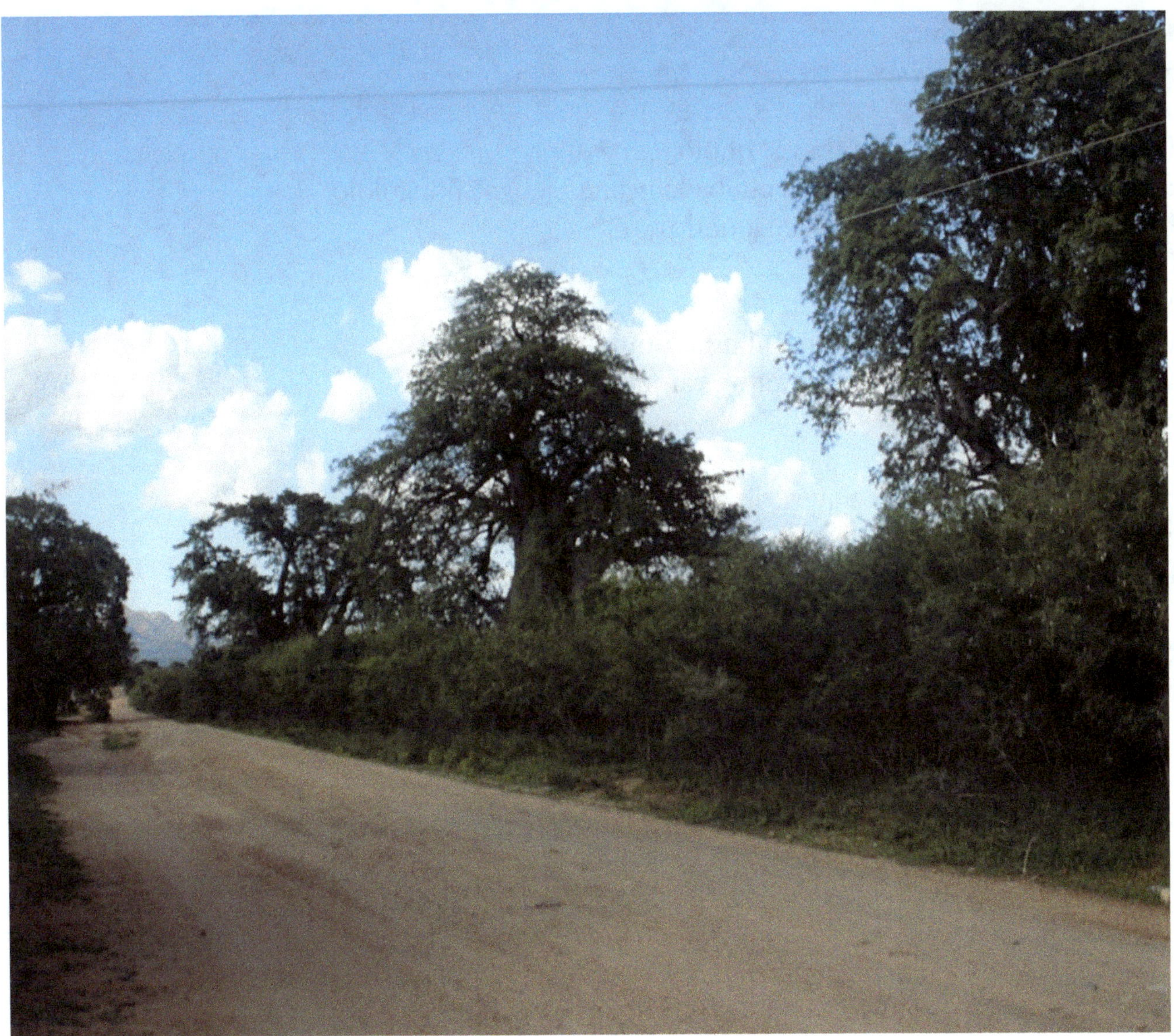

Holding the Line: The Summer After
Tendai Rinos Mwanaka

Ungazitshela ukuthi...

Ayanda Valeria Sithole

Ungamdobha ngamehlo uthi yis' qholo
Umhlube ngamagama umbona ehuba kancane njengotshongololo
Unyantikane udl' amathamb' engqondo
Uzibuze uziphendule ukuthi
Wazigqaja kangaka umuntu
Kanti ke akukho okusa ndibilitshi ngal' umuntu
Imtshaqana yamathambo enqweqwe yamuka lamayaka
Sijolozele phambili
Lapho esizahlala pekle
Kumamatheke abazali leziqu zezibeletho zethu ngobubili
Sikhombe ngophakathi
Basibuke kusigxingimfanekisomazwi
Basale bebambe owangaphansi
Ungazitshela ukuthi yibumbulu
Kanti yikuzazi lokuzethemba njengombumbulu.

Umhlab' uyahlaba

Ayanda Valeria Sithole

Indlel' ilameva
Ngiyihamba ngiphakamis ' izithende
Ubuhlungu bameva
Bugoqa inkumba igazi libe yibubende

Indlel' ilameva
Kodwa ngiyihamba ubusuku lemini
Ukusineka akukho lasemuva
Injabulo ayila mnini

Siphilela ukufa
Kukhala ozeleyo ngoba ulomlandu
Oh!
Kwaze kwazwela.

Mtanami

Ayanda Valeria Sithole

Izibulo likanina
Elimhlophe nke njengetshebetshebe yolwandle
Umazthulela njengesiziba somfula ongela kudwadla
Kuphela nje nxa engahlokozwanga
Iphupho elafika emhlabeni kungagqizwe qhakala
Yaba sisigxingi sothando lweqiniso.
Abongwe Amandla kaMvelinqangi
Avimb' izigwebo lensini zenzondo
Abongwe amandla kaThixo asungula isihlupheki
Abongwe amandla kaNkulunkulu
Aphendula inyembezi zenyumba ziwenze injabulo
Abongwe!

Impilo emnandi

Ayanda Valeria Sithole

Ngifisa ukuphila
Ukuphila nje impilo emnandi.
Impilo engela nzondo,
Impilo eholwa luthando,
Impilo ethunqa umusa,
Impilo ehlubula ukusa,
Impilo ehlambulukileyo,
Impilo ethambileyo,
Impilo engela kulamba,
Impilo engekho mnyama njenge mamba,
Impilo elephunga lamakha amnandi,
Impilo emnandi.

Siba lwami

Ayanda Valeria Sithole

Siba lwami ,
Ungacini ngokuhlanzela ogwalweni
Ngivulele iminyango okholweni
Ungicungele osizini lwenhlupheko
Engicikedela ingihlekise ngabantu.

Siba lwami lo!
Ngihlangule kuleli thala
Lomangoye olala eziko
Ngihluthune ebuhlungwini
Bokulala ngengqweqwe zomlomo.

Siba lwami,
Ngindizise njengenyoni
Unyawo olungela mpumulo
Lugxobe emazweni abendlebe zikhany' ilanga
Kujabula abazali .

Siba lwami lo!
Ngiphumelelise
Njengomzali,
Umtanami aphile impilo engcono
Engadli ngaphansi kwethala njengenja
Kodwa akhombe ngophakathi ngenxa yakho.

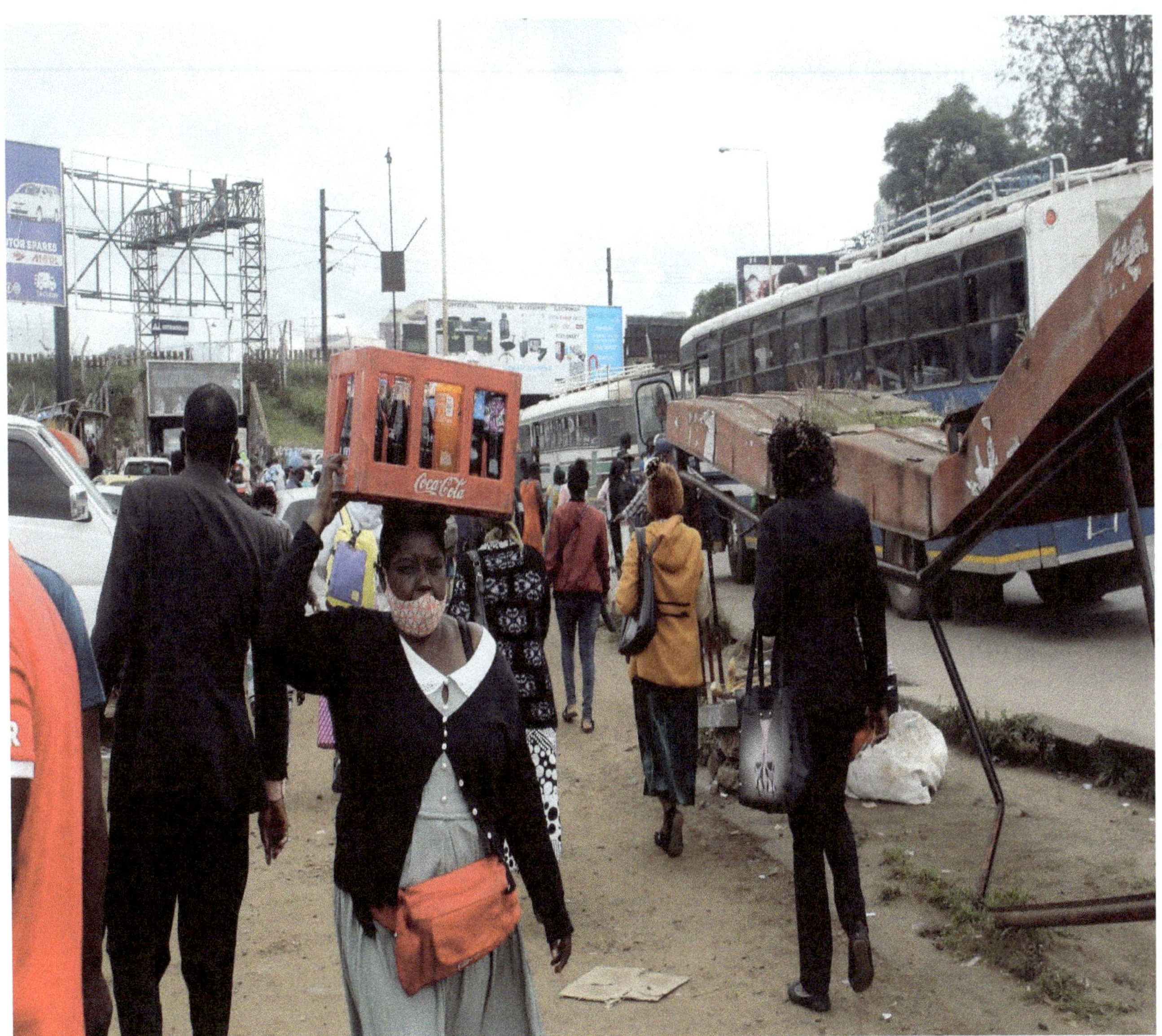

Pa Flyover
Tendai Rinos Mwanaka

Ndoshaya kuti ndodini?
Chenjerai Mhondera

Usiku ndivete, dzimwe nguva hope dzinotiza,
Pfungwa dzongova barawamhanya,
Pauri ndangariro ndiye name;
Rusero rwakunga,
Kudodziti handei, idzo tana
Dzichiti pauri dzakawana rudekaro!

Ndoshaya kuti ndodini?
Ndinomboti kwadziri dai wanomutsa wako mudiwa, umuti kuno,
Rudo semweya mutsvene rwandidzikatira,
Seshavi richiramba kutandanuka,
Sengozi rwuchindionesa ndondo,
Asi irwo rwunoti tana, kutumwa rwuchiramba!

Ndoshayiwa kuti ndodini?
Ndinomborwuti zvawadya dzangu hope,
Kuna iye mwene werudo,
wadiiko ukamurotesawo zvako dziri hope,
Uchimushapurira zviromokoto zvisina mapitse,
Kuti "wako anokuda, kana nasvai wehope adzishaya,
Pfungwa pauri dziri kurezvwa dzichiti kwaari,
Iyeyu uyu ndiye wandinoda - kureva iyewe,
Ane runako rwunopingaidza kunge gona rehuroyi,
Wakamuroya zvirikwazvo nokuti usiku haurari kumba kwako,
Kungoti kwake mumachira,

Iwe nyengu, mugota make pindikiti,
Rezano zvino haachina!"
Rwako rudo rwuchindipisa mwene sendiri muchitokisi,
Uku semurindi wejere, rwuchinditi garamo!

Ndoshayiwa kuti ndodini?
Ndinombotura befu - refu
sendinoti urinzwe kureko, kuti ubvunze,
Kuti zvaita seiko Gono
rangu, Chirandu - Moyo; iwe mufudzi nemurapi wedzangu ndangariro;
Akabata rudo rwangu nemoyo, yangu hana ikagonyevenuka?
Asi zviroto ishura rinotendwa nearota,
Kuti chakadya chakaoneka -
Chakatadzisa varume kumera mazamu pambabvu,
Ndichowo chakadya vakadzi ndebvu pamurebvu!

Asi kwandiri ndoshayiwa kuti ndodini?
Ndinomboti ndikunyorere rugwaro here?
Ndinozoti ko rwukaraviwa nemakarwe,
Ukadyiwa zvako uri mupenyu?
Ndomboti ndikurovere runhare here?
Ndozongoti ko nhamba yako zvakunongova kurova kweyangu hana;
Ndichifunga zvatichave musi waunonditi dhee kutarisa mumaziso,
Tsinga dzerudo dzichimhanya mhanya sevashandi vemuhotera,
Kuti iwe neni tiwane kudya
kunozipa nekugutsa moyo,
Yako poto yakaurungana semukaka-kora uri muhodzeko;
Ipo tichidya nemananda....
Asi dai kwaingova kudya chete, waiti Gono karume kanoruta,

Asi takatsidzirana kuti ini ndini rako dangwe negotwe,
Panoyamwa dzedu pwere, ini uchinditiwo dzokauyamwe;
Tichishapurirana dzerudo pasina mashoko;
Chinobatwa chikasadanwa nekudavira nezita,
Tichiti chine yacho midzimu
Asi uchimbova upiko mudzimu,
Usingakandiswi mapfumo pasi nerwedu rudo,
Rwunobhebha sekamoto kamberevere;
Kasingazezi matanda kupisa?

Zvandadai ndafumura hapwa;
Kuti tipotere kunyika iyo yausingaoni
Nokuti ipapa ndiri kutoshayiwa kuti ndodini?

Love steals the show

Translation by Chenjerai Mhondera

At night, sleepless I become,
Memories, fond on you,
Collected, they're -
On you entertained - finding pleasure and rest

Obsessed I am!
My command a wish
To let such love obsessive go off me,
And summon you - banging, banging and banging
Until from your sound sleep you wake too,
For you like me to experience
How so obsessive and possessive,
This love, thread-bare leaves me with no option.

But so stubborn this love is!
Mechanically it operates not so.
As it refuse to communicate the same to you my love.

I am left without option!
I know no rest,
As in my long helpless sighs and breaths,
I wish you can hear me
And to me, you pose intimate questions,
That oh what happened to you of the Heart totem -
The shepherd of my love,
And the magician of my unbridled feelings,

A beautiful memory - and health thought,
Oh you the architect of my sweet adoration?
But like a dream, everything doesn't stand to you!

I am left without option!
Scribbling you a letter, I often try,
But I fear it may end in wrong hands.
A phone call away, you're just but I can't,
as you're my very own heartbeat,
In my solitude as I ponder
What we shall be, on the day
we shall set eyes on each other;
Our arms long enough to reach you
In the physical world, our love veins,
Afforded a taste of their sweet collection,
As I come into you my virgin,
All such vows and words intimate,
Finding their perfect match in action -
A simple and single, tiny lit, setting our entire forest of love ablaze

Maybe after this explosion,
I am healed from the demon of implosion,
For all this while, I've been
neither here nor there,
Because so broke of options, I am

The done undone

Chenjerai Mhondera

The departure has come not yet,
As everything in its prayery tone,
Speak to thousand falls,
About once beautiful souls
That used to inhabit in
those mountains, yonder -
Blue with horizons,
Freezing with winter,
And beckoning with expectations...

The one plus one of life,
Gracious with meanness of answers,
Conscience mulled by wicked meditation,
In this troubled collection,
Where every delay amounts to curiosity,
Anxiety like flames raging
Like a Russian lethal rocket,
Silently sapping life from a Ukraine victim.

Dear life (In Sorrows)

Chenjerai Mhondera

My sorrows, how so sad are you
That you speak not,
When the bad happens to you?

You coil, huff, mumble,
And shy away in pain
The truth a coward, bullied and bullied,
In millions rebuffs - the high five,
A naive, tossed and hitting badly hard,
Against sanity in regrettable
in fragile collection.

My sorrows who do you fear, this much,
That you're all this alone, an alien,
In chains, bound by hurt, blurt, and farts?

My sorrows in these puffs,
Tough and rough-ridden,
You may end up being a killer!

My sorrows if you keep this
sad, who your bailer can be?
Oh hey listen, in your adamant, still this sad,
I 'll report you to happiness,
And you'll be detained in
smiles, laughter and joy;

Freeing to soul, heart and mind

Behind a Zero

Chenjerai Mhondera

I'd finished thinking about nothing
When something came to my mind,
And quizzed me that 've you
seen how important is nothing?

I was blank - completely a blackout!
Apprehended by the thought, piety
And vigilant in its demands

But I'd never seen how important is nothing,
Except in arithmetic where the zeroness of number,
Does not mean nothing
As zero is a significant figure,
Zero makes other digits live their dignity
In their multiplicity
Zero creates no room for vacuum
As zero is a place occupant

Zero makes a ten live its ten,
A hundred its hundred, a thousand its thousand,
A million its million and a billion its billion -

And ever does such without getting hurt,
Or feeling envy or jealousy

Zero is that poor son-in-law in the village,
Never short at family events as the chief organiser,
And runner for the success of the event,
But who hardly gets named when the
flashy sons-in-laws descend all the way from the city,
To give a huge impression of their presence finally,
As they steal the show.

Zero is the vigilante figure
Taking good stock of the family livestock,
And sustaining life in the village,
But seldom gets recognised
When the sons and daughters from the city
And abroad come in their elegant cars and attire

Zero makes me cry!
For Zero's story is long and sad.
He's the most aged of all his siblings -
Kiths and kins, and yet he's made to live like a junior, possessed and slave
Zero makes his brothers live large,
prosperous and up to their prospects,
But is always looked down upon, spit at,
Mocked and evil-talked

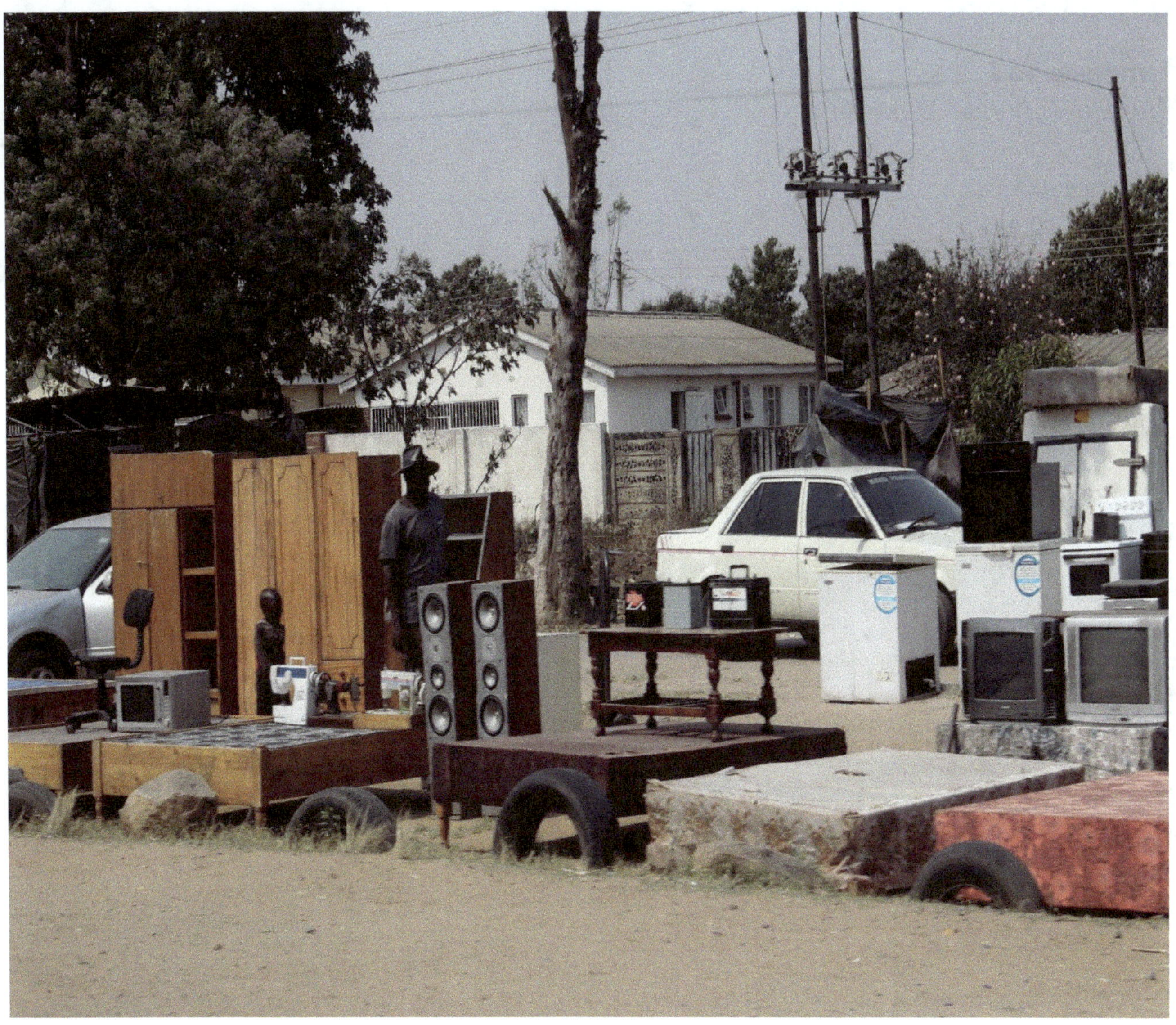

Furniture Shop
Tendai Rinos Mwanaka

Lamentations

Beniah Takunda Munengwa

Rise or fall,
Intricate spaces
All fine lines

Young or old
A whip of the air
Dull margins

Being born to die
30 years in,
Waiting to grow

Without God,
A nothing waiting
To be blown away by wind

Too many to count
A lessening of the love
Who you start with

A beginning
of an eternal pain
An undying cemetery thorny rose

Chronicles

Beniah Takunda Munengwa

Father said,
something can be broken

A brokenness
So broken
That no one can fathom

A brokenness
That can be a part of your past,

A past you cannot erase
A past that was
and a past that will always be

And that it can be said
It was you who broke the glass

And yet you were just but carrying
A broken glass, only waiting to be pieces...

Revelations

Beniah Takunda Munengwa

Writer, writer
For how many years have you emptied
Thy ink bottle,

For how many years have you?
This I ask

But your belly still knaws,
Empty
Like an unscibled epitaph

Your gift making room for you
Among great names
Great spaces

But not your belly, not your nest
Published and cited in books,
articles and newspapers
we cannot afford

And now I see, you scatter
Searching for the light,
One you can use in your homestead

...I've been one of you
And, I am now on the highway
...running

Hoping but knowing
That which heats up the heart
Might not be the one that caters for the heart to beat..

Memory Lane

Beniah Takunda Munengwa

Just a year ago,
Was a definite portrayal
Of the sweetest moments
Of a young musician like you,
The view of a rising sun,
With your music occupying
The streets, the luxurious homes
And the bathroom anthems,
Which made you to acquire
New guitar strings, and drums,
On loan, so as to supplement
Your sweet organic voice.
I can't call it a panglossian feeling,
For, with that potential,
You were going up, on an acute angle,

Such that no-one could expect a demise,
But who could defy the laws of pop-culture,
Regulations which despise quality,
So long it's not relevant to the
Present happenings.
A year later, he was in the arts graveyard,
As the crowds now knit their jerseys
Drank beer, talking
Saying that it was obvious, it could not last,

And his sound became strange orchestra
To the spaces it used to.

Epitaph
Beniah Takunda Munengwa

To you,
Nakisai

The one
Who was born

But too lazy
To wait to be able to read this

To be the big sister you were meant to be,
Getting married, growing old

And allowing us to play
With your Children

...one day you'll tell us why
You were so much in a hurry

To go to the land of another unknown,
where we could never get to let you know us..

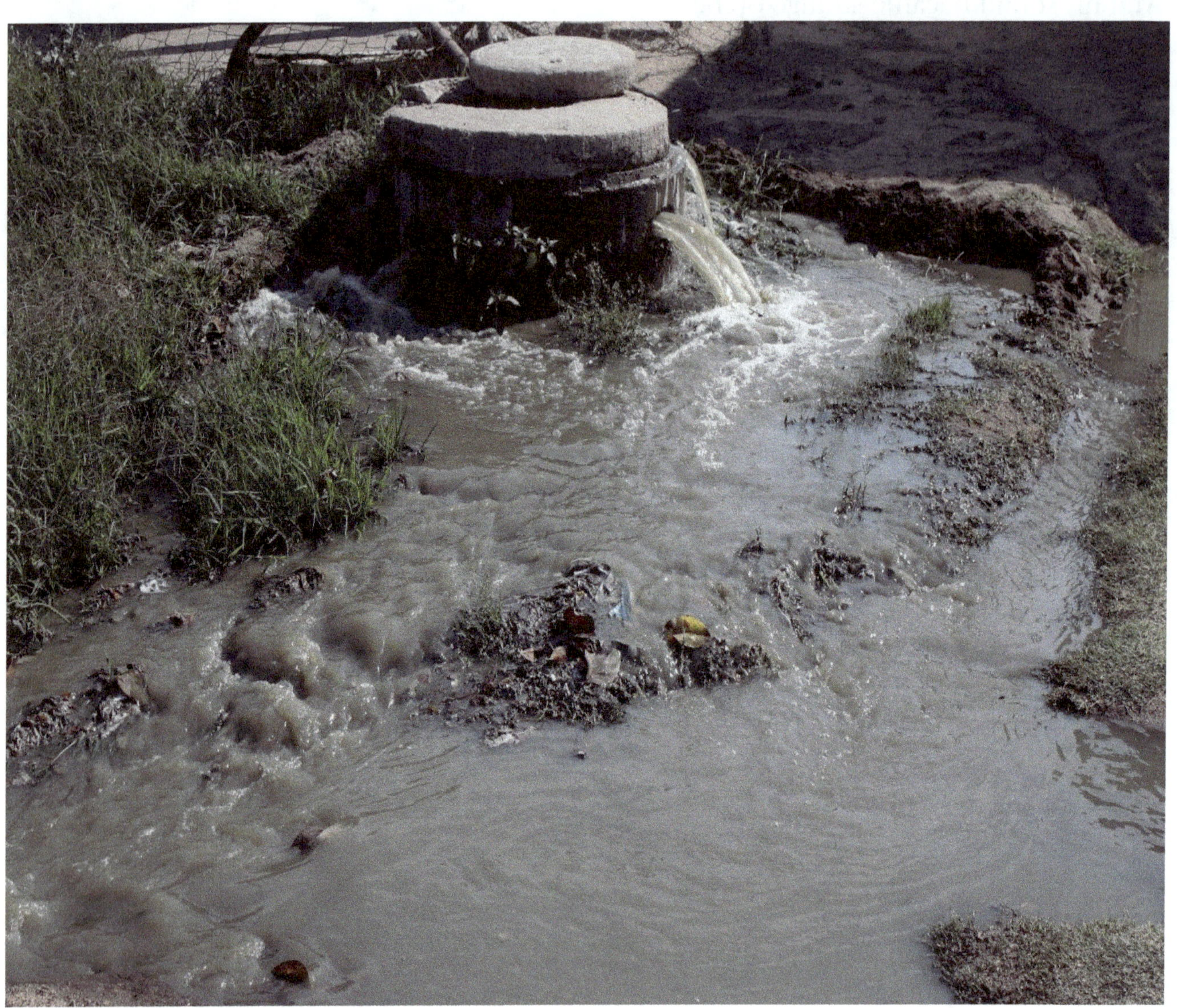

Sewage River
Tendai Rinos Mwanaka

My pride

Rejoice Tavonga Makunda

This is Zimbabwe
Dzimbadzemabwe
(houses of stone)
City of Harare being the capital
The capital
In which never sleeps
Haarare
(one doesn't sleep)
You work and never stop
That's the only way to survive
Poverty is the new norm
A full day with power
Becomes a shock
Becoming rich is witchcraft
You can't get rich in Zimbabwe
Shurugwi's quench their thirst
Using our blood
That is the new norm

This is Zimbabwe
My home and pride
Dzimbadzemabwe

My first time on stage

Rejoice Tavonga Makunda

I feel the panicked thud in my chest
The thud won't go away
My eyes browse the room
Black walls and lights only pointing one side
I can barely see where I step
I worry I shouldn't have come
I push myself though
Because this is what I want and need
Opening my heart to new experiences
Erase any hints of anthropophobia
Unlike anything I can do for the photophobia
The light blinds me as I get on stage
I start speaking I release
I am proud

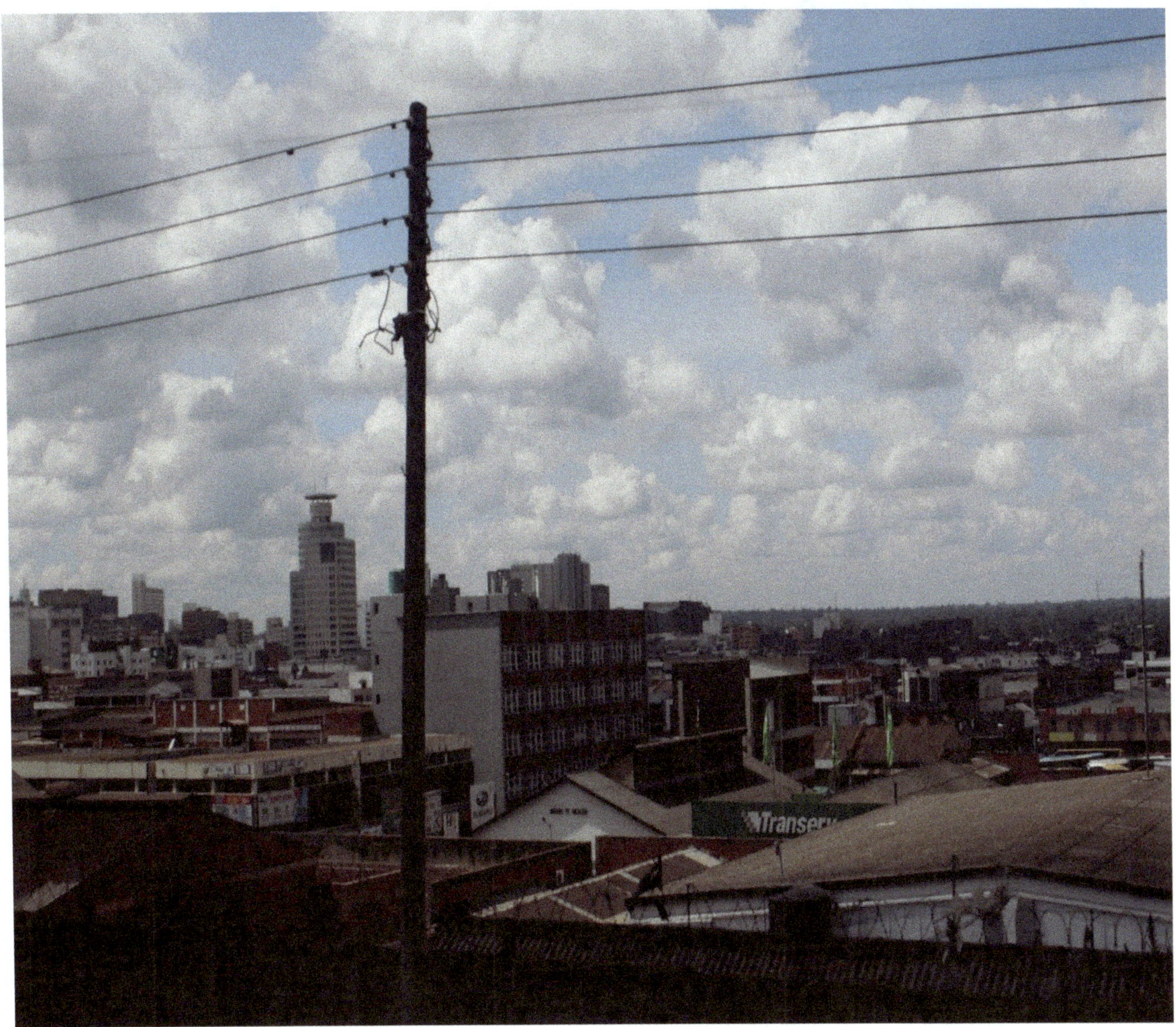

Harare, View from the Kopje
Tendai Rinos Mwanaka

Harare

Oscar Gwiriri

Good-bye sweet Harare!
I am done with your hara-kiri.
Good-bye damn Harare!
You will never see my sins again.
Good-bye darling Harare!
I will never see your scenes again.

Mirror

Oscar Gwiriri

I stuck my new mirror glass
On the blue shower walls.
I went to work for the whole day,
When back home, I was shocked
To see my mirror shattered on the floor,
And a piece was in African map shape.
I wondered if that's the sacred way
The African Continent broke off the globe.

Injured

Oscar Gwiriri

Gathering sea shells
At Beira beach,
Foreign bodies
Amongst cowries,
A broken bottle
Sliced my poor finger.
Did the ocean set me?

The bookshelf

Oscar Gwiriri

I bought this expensive bookshelf,
May I have the money to buy books.
Oh Lord, give me energy to publish my books!
Adjudicators, please nominate them for awards,
I wish to fill that shelf with book awards.
Displaying this bookshelf is my only pride.

A letter to my ex

Oscar Gwiriri

I write this short letter
With tears running up,
I can't make it long either,
As a man, I don't want
Anybody to see me in torn tears.

The sole purpose of this letter
Is just to say, I am sorry!
Since I have left and moved,
Now I realise all my damn mistakes.

I wonder how and why
You never persecuted me for my wrongs,
Now that I am in my own world,
I realise I was a bloody-damn-fool.
I am so sorry, my dear!

Putting myself in your shoes,
I wouldn't want anybody to misbehave either,
Can't withstand a such-alike tenant
Whose children graffiti painted my walls
Or damage the fittings of my house.
Thank you for your tolerance, dear landlord!

Wedding Day
Tendai Rinos Mwanaka

I find African very peaceful

David Chasumba

Smell of gunpowder across the continent
I cannot smell it,
Screams of war prisoners
I cannot hear them
I never heard the word, 'war'
Nor can I spell it
For I find African very peaceful

I don't hear the staccato
Of gun fire in Congo
Liberia, Somalia, Angola
And across the equator
Nor the shouts, 'Guns before butter!'
That nutter politicians and rebels mutter
All this doesn't matter
For I find Africa very peaceful

I haven't read of deadly missiles
Pounding cities to ruins
Nor daggers splitting skulls
Nor landmines blasting limbs
Nor looters yelling, 'A looter continua!'
While salvaging and ravaging
In the looters' paradise

I haven't seen gory images on tv

Of demented rebels wielding
Swords of Damocles
Marching into hapless villages
And butchering without mercy
Lord, I said I haven't seen such savagery
For I find Africa very peaceful
(Harare, 1997)

I feel the aura of your presence

David Chasumba

I feel the aura of your presence
Lingering beside me, near
The smell of your presence here
Like Frankincense in the air
I feel the aura of your presence
In the silence, in the absence
Making my grieving heart
Grow fonder and fonder

I see you in the shadows
Dancing around the room
Shadows dimming the light
And hovering within sight

I see you in my dreams of places
We strolled and kissed
Places we got pissed, places we strove
And made love, places we dreamed dreams
And hummed hymns

I hear your voice
Like radio waves transmitting
From far and clear
To antenna of my ear

I hear you whisper into my ear

'I still love you. Don't fear nor shed a tear.'
I feel the aura of your presence
Overwhelming me like fragrance

I talk to you everyday
When doing dishes
When dusting the den
I recount the life we shared
The vows we declared
And love words left unsaid

One day our souls will reunite
Our souls will ignite
And light the night
One day our souls will rise
In some paradise without death
Without ill-health
Without variant of virus
A paradise with just us
A second honeymoon with just us

There are still poets

David Chasumba

Though our liberators have become dictators
There are still poets…

Though our liberators have become dictators
There are still poets rhyming at this hour
Of tyrants who win at any cost
Of dictators snorting cocaine of power
And of young girls they deflower
Of liberators who have become emperors
Sitting on citadels of power
Of tyrants that do not empower
The starving masses.

Though our liberators have become dictators
There are still poets
With eyes to see tears, and ears to hear fears
Of the oppressed masses.

Though our liberators have become emperors
There are still poets to witness, as they must
The hour when emperors stumble
When citadels of power crumble
When dictators return to dust.

N.B: This poem by David Chasumba originally appeared in the now discontinued online journal, Mosi oa Tunya Review, Issue 2.

The Mayor's Children
David Chasumba

Feral children with keys to Harare city
A bustling city without pity
Feral children window-shopping in malls
And roaming through parks and city halls
Barefooted and penniless children
Too tired of crawling down drainpipes
And straying through alleys in town
Feral children too tormented by destitution
And too vulnerable to exploitation
Feral children who mastered the art
Of begging a stranger for a nut
Thin urchins with taut bellies
Skinny urchins who never go without
Rummaging for Sadza morsels
Bread, chicken wings, black bananas, beans
Cherries and berries in black bins
Children initiated into kidulthood
And eking a living in this concrete jungle
Where survival of the meanest is the jingle.

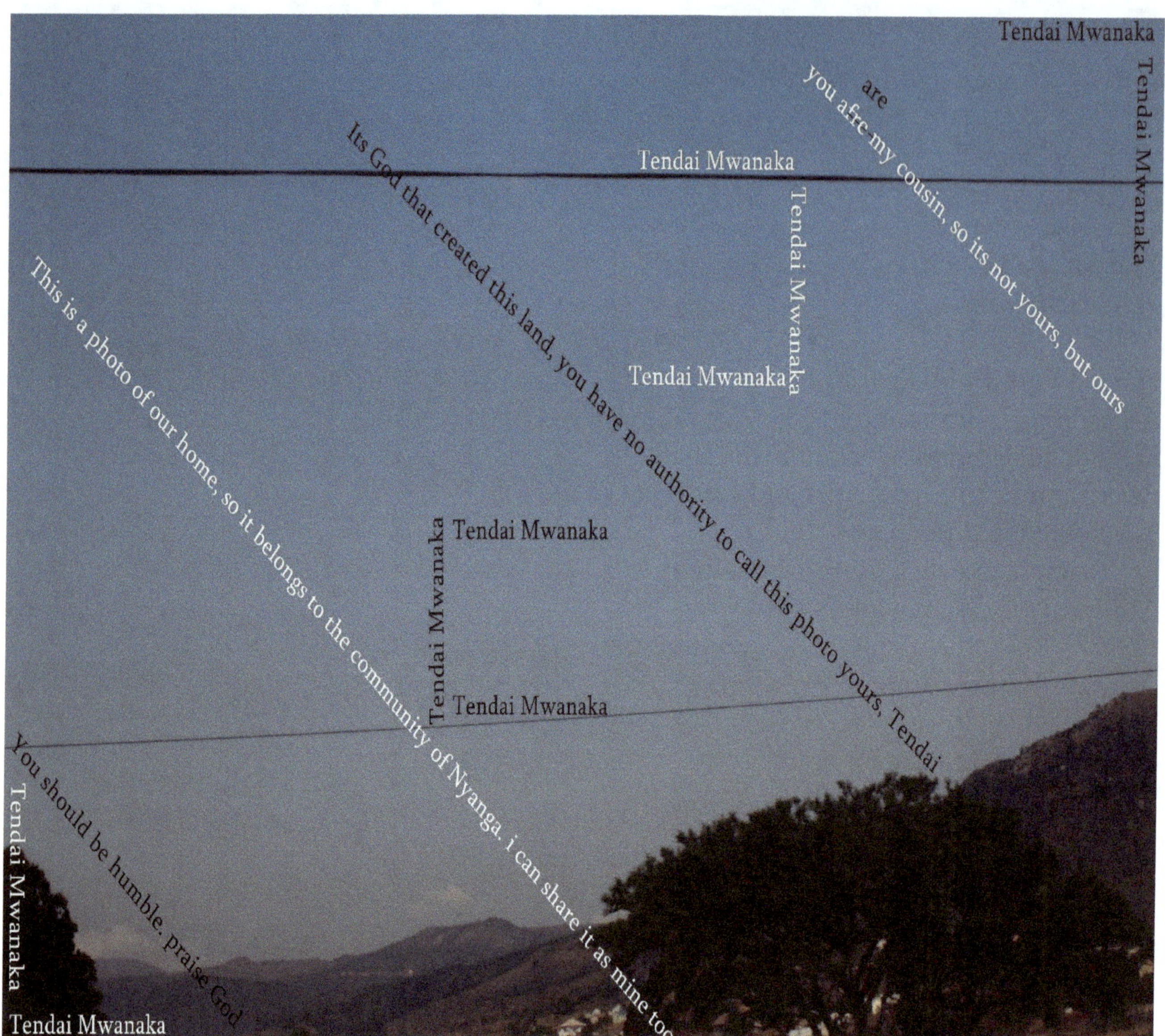

This Photo is not Mine
Tendai Rinos Mwanaka

The Lady In Red

Panashe Goneso

Her head bound in a black doek,
Her conscience screams out like a siren.
Telling her to take a stand
Against the injustice dealt her.
But whenever she tries to,
she cowers.

Ronald stands in front.
She behind Ronald, hand in hand
As Ronald leads her on....
On to sophisticated social gatherings, and her demise.

dressed in red,
the lady in red stands irresolute
not sure of her place.
her red dress garners for attention
dressing down her depression.
the lady in red
much like a backdrop
plays her role all too well.

The perfect wife to Ronald...
make-up masking her misery
she plays her role all too well.

her neck adorned by pearls,

she resembles someone sophisticated, serene.
But the pearls feel like a hangman's knot.....
and she enjoys it.

the lady in red.
she ought to draw...
Attention
Appreciation
and Affection.

But now,
the lady in red lacks energy, passion and danger.
Now she follows ~ruler~ Ronald
and depends on Ronald's counsel.

she was the lady in red.

Old Chipare

Panashe Goneso

Old Chipare
Was a man
Of the Old Order
Who lived life to the full.

He was the one
Who taught me profane jokes
Hurling obscenities back and forth.
He cautioned me
To never share my jokes
Until I belonged to the Old Order.

Old Chipare used to sit
On his favorite spot
Under the gnarled and sapless Musasa,
A reflection of him.

He was the one
Who told me of the comforting warmth between a woman's thighs
Never caring to dress up his words
Which sounded obscene to my virgin ears.
He warned me
Not to be enslaved
By the power which a woman has
Between her thighs

Old Chipare is now gone
A certain life seems to have gone with him
Even the Musasa seems to have grown older
But when the wind rustles its leaves,
I hear Old Chipare laughing.

Deep in the wee hours

Panashe Goneso

I toiled and wrestled
Sleep evaded me
As I worked to make worth of my words.
A random burst of energy flowing through me,
I felt rejuvenated...
My creative juices flowing like the currents of the Great Save in her former glory,
I typed and typed and typed...
But I could bring no meaning to my words.
The flow of my current was choked by a dam of self-doubt, inconsistency
But still....
I groveled til I made sense of my words.
And like a butterfly emerging from the cocoon,
my toiling finally came to fruition,
in the early hours of the morning...
with the rising of the sun.
The dam broke...
and with it, my field was replenished.
And so I worked
feeling relieved.
Anticipating the foreplay of wordplay,
enjoying the mental orgasm of malapropisms ...
slowly building up to a rich climax .

Silently aggressive,
DO NOT BE PENSIVE!
but rather be attentive and listen to this missive

Eerie times we live in,
where crimes are thriving
And Lady Justice seems to be blindfolded to the calls of justice

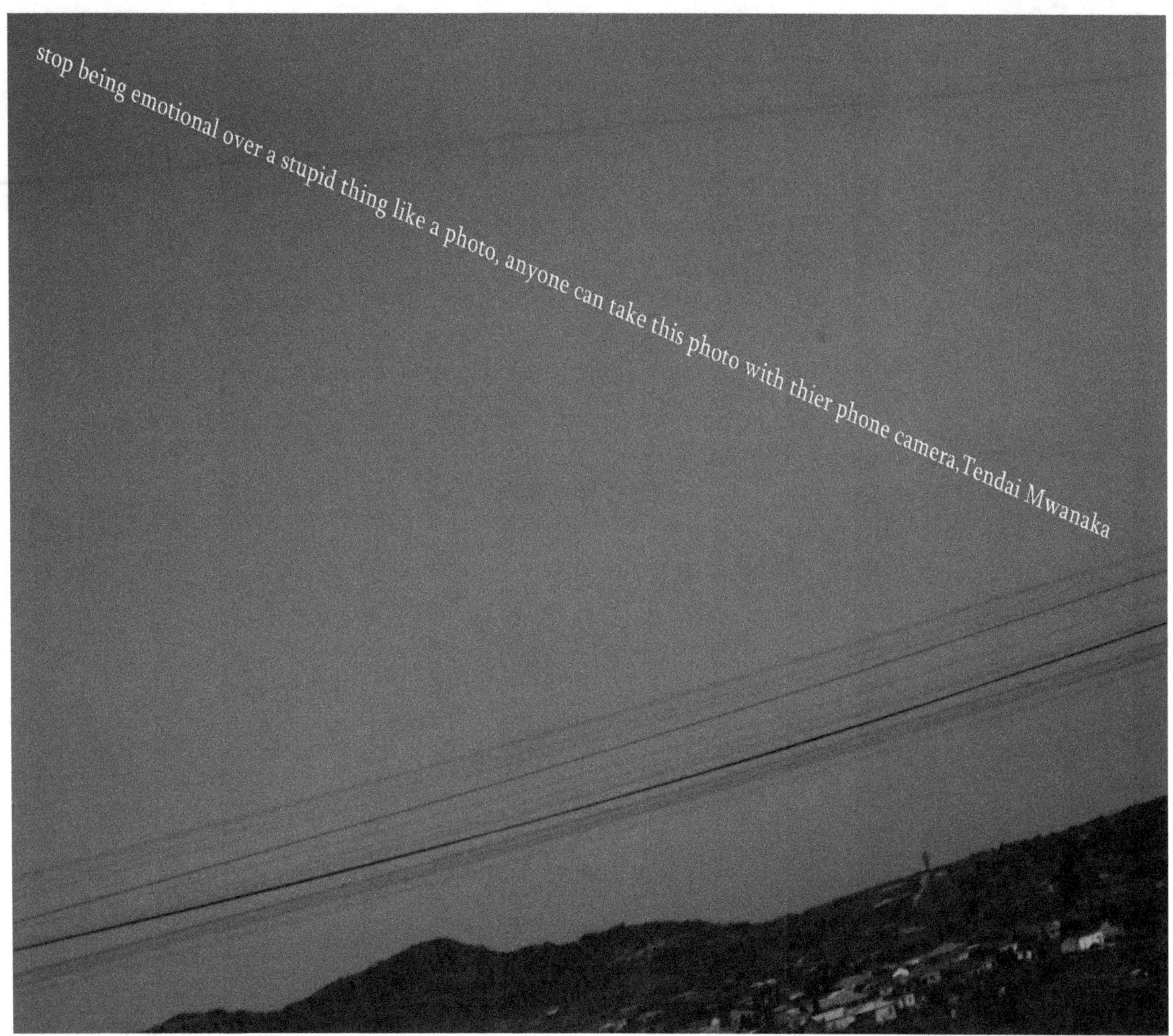

Justification for piracy
Tendai Rinos Mwanaka

Hallucinations

Gamuchirai Susan Muchirahondo

I want you to hold me like you do that coffee mug in your hands
Skimming over the porcelain like an enchanted vase
I wanted you to call my name
In the dark and tell me to wait
I did still
For you

I have memories of us that never occurred
Were we not in the garden together this past summer?
Did you not tame my heart with abundance?
The gentleness that I fought off with all my might
That I couldn't fight any longer

Did you not calm my rage with gentle head rubs and shoulder brushes?
Did you not take me away from the noise to silence my fears
The anxiety that wore me that day like a coat on winter mornings?
Did you not hold my face in your hands and tell me it was going to be okay?

Did you not exist on that porch bench with me and light up the apartments with your beautiful taste in music?
Did you not teach me patience in the desperate moments?
Did I not fall deeper and deeper?

With my fantasy?

Perhaps you really didn't exist.

I never did anyway.

Old Friend

Gamuchirai Susan Muchirahondo

There are moments that steal into my memory
I have been holding on to all these beautiful things for over a year now
Eating with my mouth and not my phone
I have been away from the ink and paper
Away from all kinds of head trauma

It's strange to see you again
Old friend,
How have you been?
I am not broken
Did you hear that?

I somehow got better
I met strangers that changed my life
I met friends and decided to stay this time
How have you been?
Still silent in the broken house by the corner?

Come out.

We've found light.
We've found love, my love.

I packed all my bags and moved into a new state
I have not been that deeply sad for a while
I made it out alive somehow
I found life somehow

Old friend

I am writing poetry out of inspiration, again now
I do not bleed through ink
I do not die page by page anymore
I bought a book
To read.

I spend time with my family
I have new family
I somehow blossomed into a being teeming with life from the edge of that cliff
Dear friend
Look at me, I'm a real life girl now

Kindled

Gamuchirai Susan Muchirahondo

I have been warned of my nature
Told to calm down so many times

Apparently

I possess too much energy to exist uniformly

That's true

They say high highs are trouble
Oh lord, since I was a kid I was told to box in my fireworks

Allowed to cracker on birthdays and maybe put on a display around the holidays

They warned me I'd crush from my highs

I suppose, they were afraid of falling.

I knew no such fear, but they imparted it on me

And so I kept all my colours inside
I kept my fireworks in the box and stayed away from ignition

But

Ignition was everywhere

In a perfectly balanced daisy
In water bubbles and florescent lights
In rainbows and clear skies
In dark clouds and thunder
In T squares and pencils
In lines and circles
In yellow
In orange
In watermelons
In breathing

And so I held my breath
For years
I held it so closely to myself and wouldn't show anyone
I wouldn't tell anyone

I secretly chased the cliffs and the freefall swings
I chased forbidden lands in secret and beamed
I beamed in quiet places no one existed

I have never been afraid of falling.
My fear of heights developed after nightmares of being held back by my world.

But that was a while ago
I found sun
I found ignition by continuing to exist
I burst into bright displays and strangers marveled at my works
And so I ran into forlorn crowds

I showed them my colours and sparkled so brightly they wore shades to see me

In the strangest places and people
I found some kind of permission
To exist
As fire
As a flame
As a collection of fireworks

And now there I go
High in my highs
Wary hearts waiting to catch me
Ready hands coming after me in dread
But I go on and on

I'm not afraid of falling
To the lowest of lows
I know it can't possibly be safe down there
But if I'm built to sparkle so much
Is there a doubt in any universe that I won't rise from a fall?

If it's possible to fall from such highs, it MUST be possible to rise from the lowest of lows

And I did
And I do.
I rise and I shine and I beam and I

Light up the skies with colour and condensations of energy

Apparently

Gamuchirai Susan Muchirahondo

They look at me like I'm a mad woman
It's not the first time I've been deemed alien because of my choices
Life
My life
They want me to live a life they would like me to have

But my shoes

These are my shoes
I wear them
I have worn them for the past two decades and more
And yet
Entitled
Here they stand to tell me

That
Maybe I'm not sure
Maybe I'm not certain
It can't possibly be
That this could be what I want

Because of course
They know me better than me
They live this life for me
And when I live how they want me to live
They'll take up the cross for me

Malicious entitlement to my destiny

Apparently I am incapable of making the right choices for myself
Apparently they know everything about me and what's best for me

Apparently

They know better.

Legend

Gamuchirai Susan Muchirahondo

You are somewhere on the horizon
I don't doubt your existence though I sometimes grow impatient
You are somehow embedded on the core of my being

A glimmering hope that I even tried to ward off
With smoking walls
I tried so hard to bury your light in the depths of despair

But you are much too hopeful
Much too powerful
And much too magnetic to this heart of mine that can't seem to erase you

A love that does not look sideways
A love that holds on as much as I have to the hope of us
A love tender and sincere

You are a dream to so many
A nightmare of loss to few
And yet you show up as mine and a beacon shining on the mountain top

You have dedicated yourself to haunting me
I have dedicated myself to believing in you
And only the universe awaits our reunion

Because I must have met you somewhere before

As I can't seem to erase you from my ore
A treasure composite of our strife and delusion.

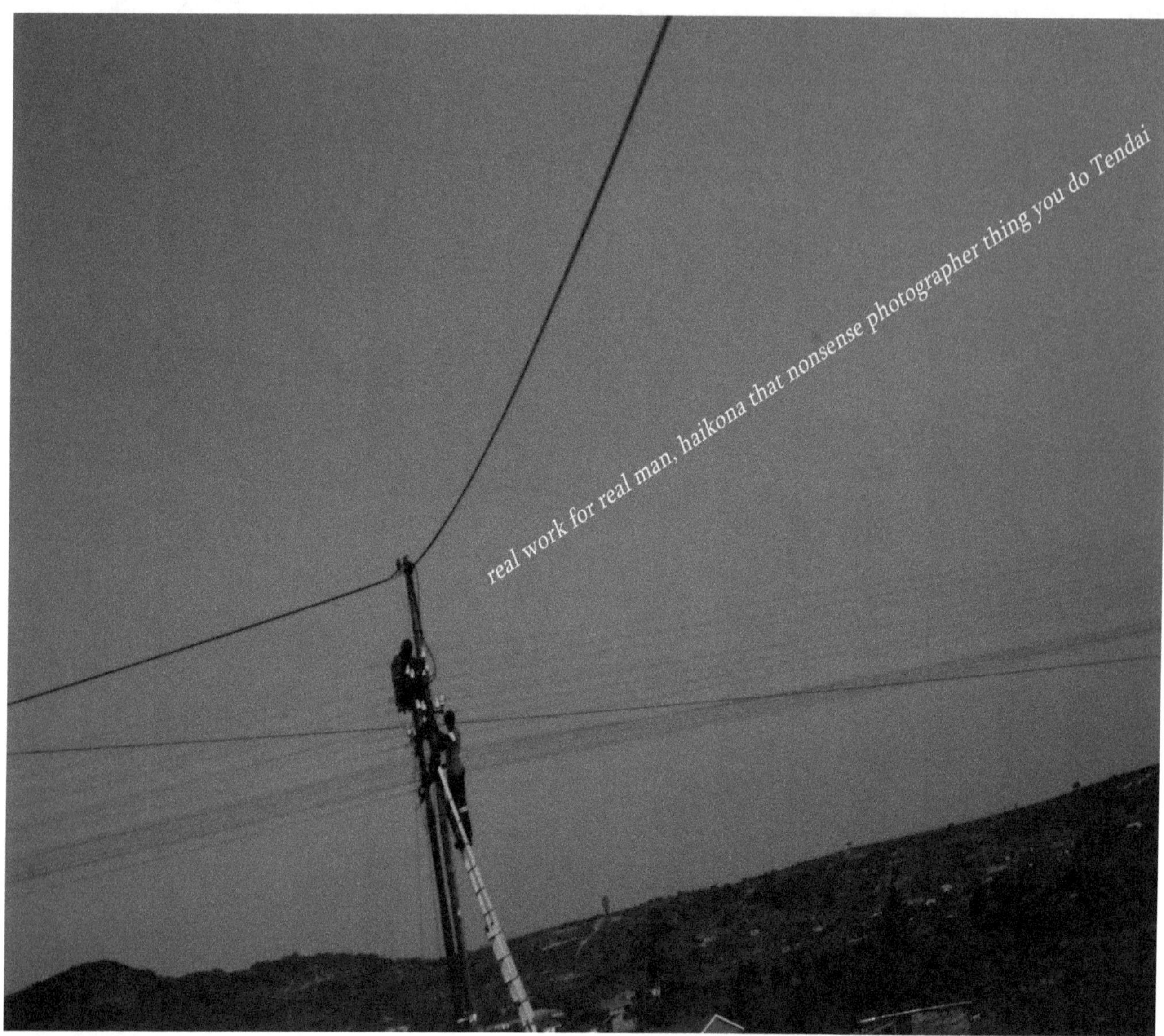

Real Work For Real Men

Tendai Rinos Mwanaka

Abortion

Bradley Nsukuzokuduma Moyo

Without a name;
sometimes I wonder what do babes do in ancestral land ?

How are they addressed, do they have peers,
do they even become ancestors ,
are they welcomed,
Do they Rest In Peace?

Sometimes I wonder what happens to dumped babies I mean fetus carcasses.

How does it feel to end an innocent life, sorry I mean an embryo.
How does God feel when you return his gift, I mean a mistake.
Do not keep quiet I am just trying to understand.

Pardon me,
I tend to forget;
You are too scared, you are not ready.

Please do not get wrong.
I am not trying to judge you
but sometimes I just wonder ,
I really wonder.
How it is that today you carry a baby and tomorrow a tomb,
How do you live with that?

We never knew dad

Bradley Nsukuzokuduma Moyo

We never knew dad
So when he died we did not cry,
He was already late before he died

Before he died, he could sleep holding his beer,
Dead drunk.
If ever there was a thing that dad held tight,
It was a cigarette, a bottle of beer
or a pair of fists that landed on the wall, the dog, mom or me.

We never knew dad,
Mother made sure we never saw him,
She was ashamed of his drinking
Or the printing he did on her face
maybe she was protecting us
Or was she protecting him?

We never knew dad,
He never bothered to know us,
Even though I had his name.

Mother always says he was a kind and loving man,
She even smiles but I am not convinced.
Her tears betray her,
She is not convinced either.

My young brothers and sisters believe this lie,
They were too young to understand.

Bastards or orphans,
The difference is the same.
Father was short, he loved shots,
His temper was short
And gladly his life was short too.

What else do I know about father?
What is there to remember,
What shall I tell my children his grandchildren?
For besides this,
We never knew father.

I once had a French lover.

Bradley Nsukuzokuduma Moyo

I once had a French lover
"Merci beaucoup, bonjour"
She introduced me to French cuisine and wines,
Paris was the dream.

I once had a French lover,
She could not pronounce my name
But loved joining it with hers
My mother thought I was crazy,
I was madly in love.

My lover was perfect
But her world was wild,
Her father; my father in law was a woman,
We addressed him in plural.

I once had a French lover,
She was my world but she also wanted the universe
And that I could not offer,
I also could not bed her well,
She wanted me to compete with her toys.

I once had a French lover,
My friends tease me about it,
Now that I think about it,
I laugh, maybe I was crazy

But I once had a French lover.

Mother

Bradley Nsukuzokuduma Moyo

She is Mine for her love is golden,
Or maybe the M stands for Merciful
But not when she is sparing the rod and spoiling the child.

The O maybe stands for Original,
Her original touch and key that shusshes the baby to sleep,
Her touch that turns meals to delicacies,
I don't even envy the fancy restaurants and hotels.

The T in mother is for the Tea she shares with her friends online,
The spill about whose husband is cheating,
whose weave to laugh about
Or maybe it stands for treasured and trusted,
I mean, don't we all trust her.

The H in mother stands for Home,
You can't convince me otherwise.
Yes she's a helper, a heroine and all
But what's a home without mother.

I am still looking for the meaning of E,

I thought it was Eternal,
Until I saw her in a coffin
And I had to realise,
I realized that the R stands for Rest in peace.

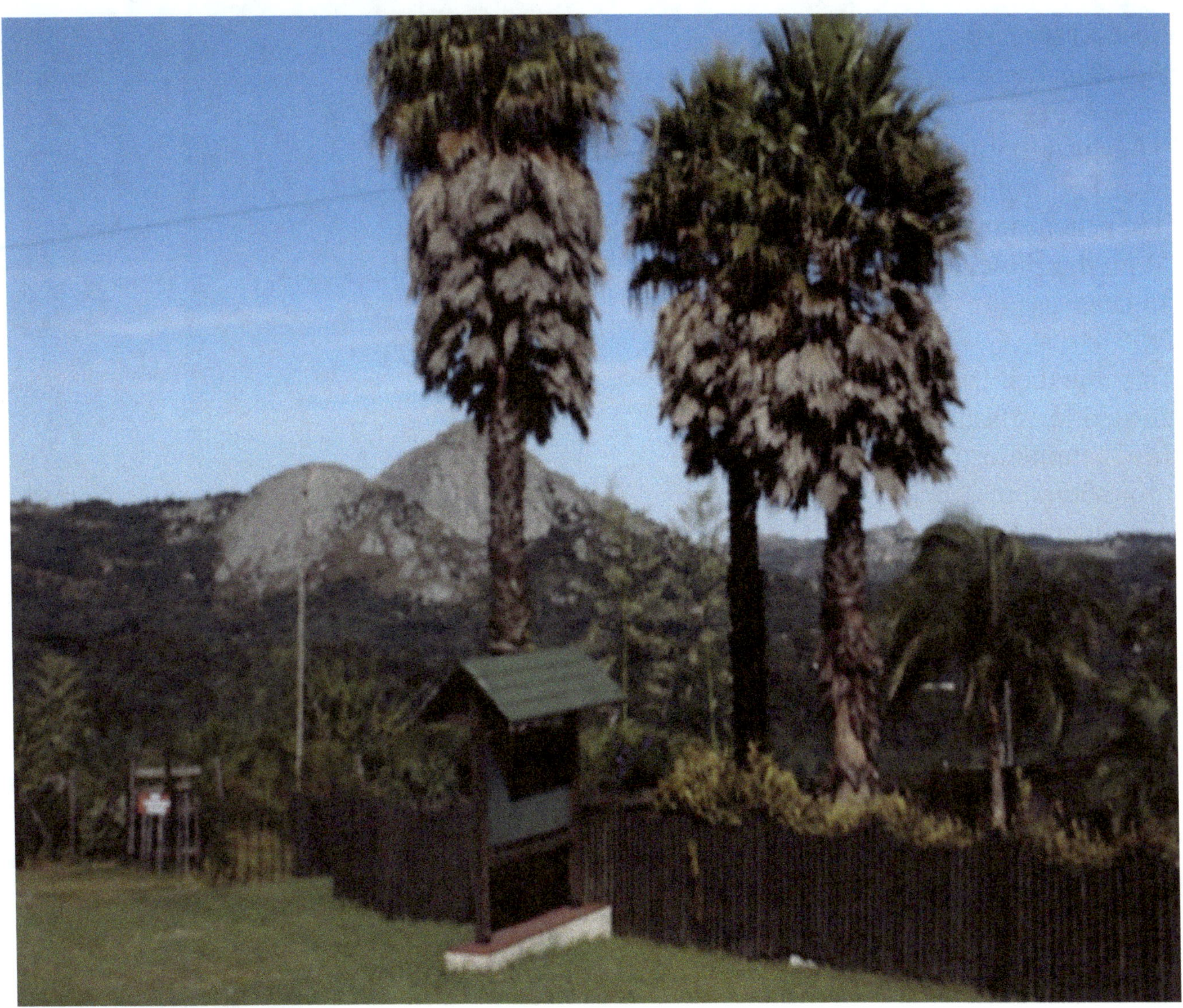

Monte Clair, Juliasdale
Tendai Rinos Mwanaka

Second Routing

Jabulani Mzinyathi

They had to ward off
Ward off tropical diseases
They then subjugated us
With the Bible, bullet and gun
In language, dress... we aped them

In come their friends from the east
Invited for so-called mega deals
Just a euphemism for enslavement
Our natural resources going for a song
The unemployed driven into slavery
Nothing to show but just a pittance

Operating under shrouds of secrecy
The owners of wealth dehumanised
Sold by the elite getting the gains
Nagasaki and Hiroshima will be child's play
When the potency of the poisoning sets in.

The Investors

Jabulani Mzinyathi

Not with shackles and chains
No longer going across the seas
Dead bodies not thrown to sharks
Right here on the African continent
Joseph still sold by his brothers
Yesterday it was the white or pink man
Today the slit eyed heartless yellow man
Call it xenophobia but it is that indignation
That righteous indignation against evil
All that remains are the poisoned rivers
The cyanide and mercury poisoned streams
All we are left with are death laden wells
Our brothers and sisters sell us into slavery
With their concubines in tow off they fly
Off to France, Malaysia, Dubai just for leisure
Off they fly to China, India and Singapore
Leaving us to die of curable, multiple diseases.
We are being sold for them to be in mansions
While we are drowning in seas of poverty
All they do is flaunt shameless profligacy

Burial Ground

Jabulani Mzinyathi

The myth of invincibility
Reduced to smithereens
The sycophants put to shame
For their talk of immortality
Born of woman he departed
Leaving the empty shells at home
The multitudes without medical care
The sun then set in Singapore
That precedent was then set
The profligacy is put on display
Flying first class to seek treatment
Only to return as mortal cargo
That one shunned that acre for reasons
All that is wrapped in the vile veil of secrecy
The gullible are then bussed to the acre
Sending off the remains of another landlord
The propaganda machinery at full throttle
Spin doctors unleash tale upon warped tale
Tales of alleged consistency and persistence
Unwavering commitment to that sacred struggle
Of liberating the masses wallowing in neglect
Another narrative will then be spun again
History is indeed the tyrant's mistress.

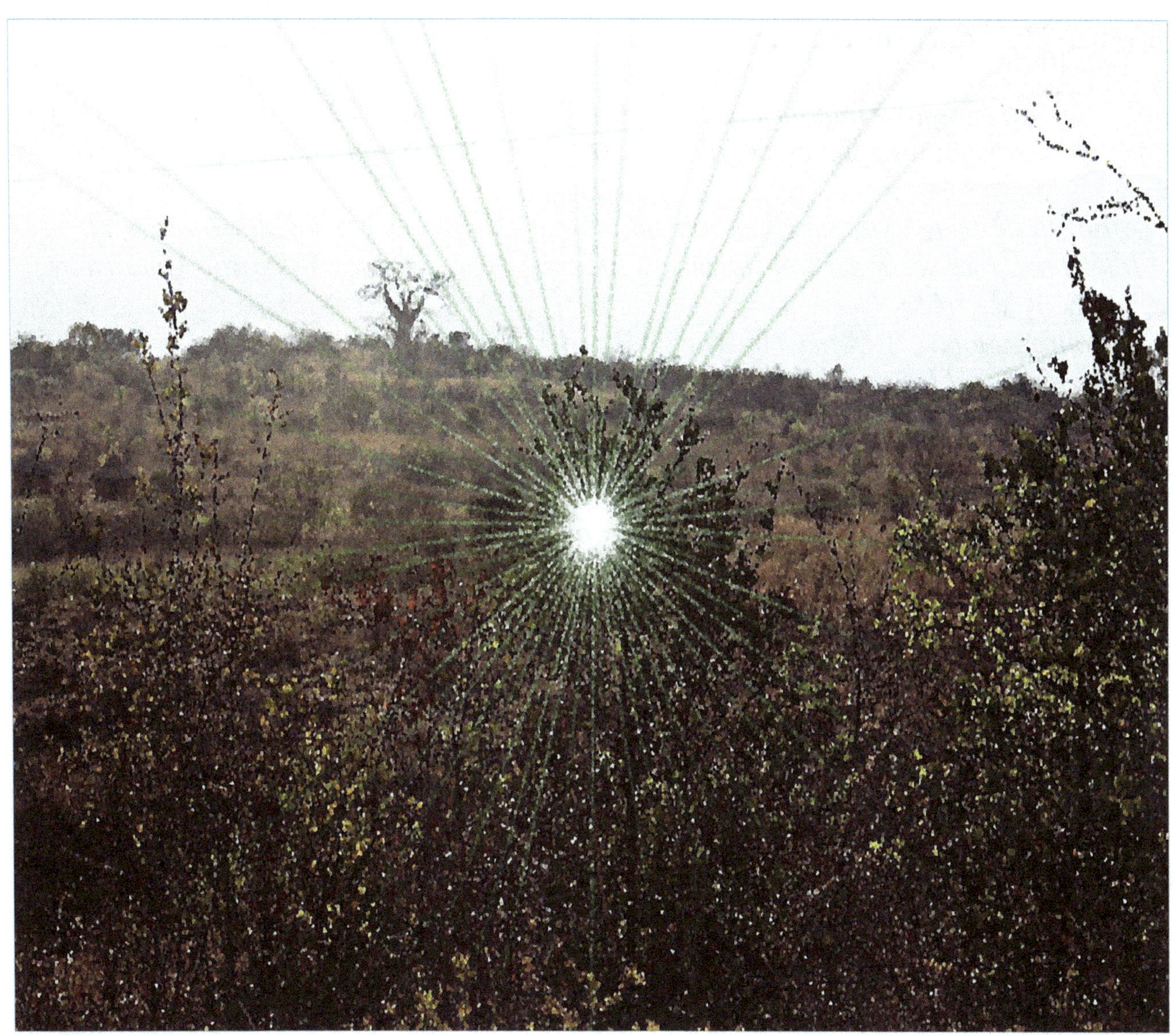

Shattered Illusion
Tendai Rinos Mwanaka

Mmap Multi-disciplinary Series

If you have enjoyed *Zimbolicious Anthology Vol 9,* consider these other fine books in the **Mmap Multi-disciplinary Series** from *Mwanaka Media and Publishing:*

Africanization and Americanization Anthology Volume 1, Searching for Interracial, Interstitial, Intersectional and Interstates Meeting Spaces, Africa Vs North America by Tendai R Mwanaka
A Conversation..., A Contact by Tendai Rinos Mwanaka
Africa, UK and Ireland: Writing Politics and Knowledge Production Vol 1 by Tendai R Mwanaka
Writing Language, Culture and Development, Africa Vs Asia Vol 1 by Tendai R Mwanaka, Wanjohi wa Makokha and Upal Deb
Zimbolicious: An Anthology of Zimbabwean Literature and Arts, Vol 3 by Tendai Mwanaka
Drawing Without Licence by Tendai R Mwanaka
Writing Grandmothers/ Escribiendo sobre nuestras raíces: Africa Vs Latin America Vol 2 by Tendai R Mwanaka and Felix Rodriguez
Tiny Human Protection Agency by Megan Landman
Ghetto Symphony by Mandla Mavolwane
A Portrait of Defiance by Tendai Rinos Mwanaka
Nationalism: (Mis)Understanding Donald Trump's Capitalism, Racism, Global Politics, International Trade and Media Wars, Africa Vs North America Vol 2 by Tendai R Mwanaka
Ouafa and Thawra: About a Lover From Tunisia by Arturo Desimone
Zimbolicious: An Anthology of Zimbabwean Literature and Arts, Vol 4 by Tendai Mwanaka and Jabulani Mzinyathi
Chitungwiza Mushamukuru Anthology by Tendai Rinos Mwanaka
The Day and the Dweller: A Study of the Emerald Tablets by Jonathan Thompson

Zimbolicious: An Anthology of Zimbabwean Literature and Arts, Vol 5 by Tendai Mwanaka
Robotics Anthology, Africa vs Asia Vol 2 by Tendai Rinos Mwanaka
Shaping Up by Tendai Rinos Mwanaka
Zimbolicious Anthology Vol 6: An Anthology of Zimbabwean Literature and Arts by Tendai Rinos Mwanaka and Chenjerai Mhondera
Registers of Loss: PhotoTalking to the Baobab Trees of Nyatate by Tendai Rinos Mwanaka
The Trick is to Keep Breathing: Covid 19 Stories From African and North American Writers, vol 3 by Tendai Rinos Mwanaka
Fixing Earth: An Anthology of Ireland, UK and Africa Writers, Vol 2 by Tendai Rinos Mwanaka
Zimbolicious: An Anthology of Zimbabwean Literature and Arts, Vol 7 Tendai Rinos Mwanaka and Tanaka Chidora
Writing Woman Anthology: Personal Essays and Short stories, An Anthology of African and Asian Writers, Vol 3 by Tendai Rinos Mwanaka, Abigail George, Sue Zhu and Monalisa Jena
Writing Woman Anthology: Drama and Scholarly Essays, An Anthology of African and Asian Writers, Vol 3 by Tendai Rinos Mwanaka, Abigail George, Sue Zhu and Monalisa Jena
WRITING WOMAN ANTHOLOGY: Poetry and Visual art by Tendai Rinos Mwanaka, Abigail George, Sue Zhu and Monalisa Jena
Zimbolicious: An Anthology of Zimbabwean Literature and Arts, Vol 8 by Tendai Rinos Mwanaka and Matthew Kunashe Chikono
Of poets, gods, ghosts. Irritants and storytellers by Tendai Rinos Mwanaka
The Aporia of Unnamed Things by Tendai Rinos Mwanaka
Glyphs of Love by Tendai Rinos Mwanaka

Upcoming

Men: An Anthology of African and Latin American writers vol 3 by Tendai Rinos Mwanaka and Ingrid Bringas

https://facebook.com/MwanakaMediaAndPublishing/

www.ingramcontent.com/pod-product-compliance
Lightning Source LLC
LaVergne TN
LVHW081251100826
845148LV00009B/1198

9781779345431